Wallace Stevens Revisited

Twayne's United States Authors Series

Joseph M. Flora, General Editor

University of North Carolina at Chapel Hill

TUSAS 617

WALLACE STEVENS
Reproduced by permission of the Huntington Library, San Marino, California

Wallace Stevens Revisited
"The Celestial Possible"

Janet McCann

Texas A&M University

Twayne Publishers
An Imprint of Simon & Schuster Macmillan
New York

Prentice Hall International
London   Mexico City   New Delhi   Singapore   Sydney   Toronto

Twayne's United States Authors Series No. 617

Wallace Stevens Revisited: "The Celestial Possible"
Janet McCann

From *Collected Poems* by Wallace Stevens.
Copyright © 1954 by Wallace Stevens.
Reprinted by permission of Alfred A. Knopf, Inc. and Faber and Faber Ltd.
From *Opus Posthumous*, edited by Samuel French Morse.
Copyright © 1957 by Elsie Stevens and Holly Stevens.
Reprinted by permission of Alfred A. Knopf, Inc. and Faber and Faber Ltd.

Twayne Publishers
An Imprint of Simon & Schuster Macmillan
866 Third Avenue
New York, N.Y. 10022

Library of Congress Cataloging-in-Publication Data

McCann, Janet.
    Wallace Stevens revisited : "the celestial possible" / Janet
McCann.
        p.   cm. — (Twayne's United States authors series : TUSAS 617)
    Includes bibliographical references and index.
    ISBN 0–8057–7644–3
    1. Stevens. Wallace, 1879–1955—Criticism and interpretation.
    2. Metaphysics in literature. I. Title. II. Series.
    PS3537.T4753Z6777   1995
    811'.52—dc20   95–13121
                                                                                      CIP

For Hugh McCann,
and in memory of
Edmund M. Lacey, 1913–1988
Pauline Hanschitz Lacey, 1916–1986

Contents

Preface

The poem must resist the intelligence
Almost successfully. . . .

"Man Carrying Thing"

Wallace Stevens's poetry is about resistance; it is both description and demonstration of the will to understand. The mind would comprehend, and the world resists. From his *Harmonium* poems on, Stevens's work presents two forces in conflict. These are identified differently in the various phases of his intellectual life, but they always represent the force within and the force without, the "lion in the lute" and the "lion locked in stone" of "The Man with the Blue Guitar." Only rarely are these forces at rest or reconciled, and then only tentatively or hypothetically. In most of the work, the mind attempts to subjugate or penetrate the real. This attempt to appropriate reality is changed, in some of the later poems, to a yielding to a transformed, reenvisioned reality, so that creation and discovery become one act. This study is an attempt to trace the shifting definitions of Stevens's two conflicting forces and to read, or reread, some of the poems in the light of these definitions.

Stevens is not assignable. He does not belong to a particular group, although he shows the influence of romantics, imagists, symbolists, and all the various schools of art and philosophy current at the century's beginning. At the same time, Stevens was nostalgic and avant-garde; he read French works too new to have been translated while claiming he longed for eighteenth-century *raffinement*. He was both elitist and proletarian, mourning contemporary commonness and vulgarity while expressing pleasure at finding butchers and farmers among his Pennsylvania Dutch ancestors. Both Mary and Martha, he preached and practiced the work ethic as well as the contemplative life. The simultaneous presence of mutually exclusive opposites was as common to his life as to his work. His life project was dealing with them as a poet and as a man.

The underlying premise of this study is that the interplay of forces in Stevens's work reflects a lifelong search for a new metaphysic, a replacement for the Christianity he discarded in his youth. The intellectual rigor of this search as Stevens interrogated, modified, and discarded various substitutes for the Christian God infuses his poetry with its characteristic intensity. Religion in all its manifestations became his major metaphor and, finally, his major subject. His substitute myths or "fictions" included forms of Buddhism, Heideggerian phenomenology, Jungian psychology, process philosophy, Nietzschean Dionysianism, and other forms of mysticism. His deathbed conversion to Roman Catholicism comes then as no surprise; he was not forced to sign on the line by zealous nuns, and his conversion certainly was not, as Joan Richardson suggests in the conclusion of her biography, a "prank." His poetry claims in its various engagements that the poet will believe in nothing less than God. Each of the substitutes, each attempt to approach the "supreme fiction," proves to be something less than God— and thus is discarded.

This direction of analysis goes against much of the New Historicist and Marxist Stevens criticism, which tend to define him both as a realist-materialist and as a product of his time. James Longenbach, Alan Filreis, and others give us a Stevens firmly grounded in his place and occupation. My perspective is more in line with studies by Joseph Carroll and Barbara Fisher, which focus on the mystical and Christian directions and influences. I argue that in addition to his constant preoccupation with things of the spirit, Stevens's career was marked by a progression toward the metaphysical. His letters as well as his poems show the degree of his concern with religion as he strips away the vestiges of childhood belief in *Harmonium*, approaches atheism in *The Man with the Blue Guitar*, and then turns toward a revitalized religious inquiry in the later poems. His last poems show his gradual approach to the religious commitment that took place at the margin of his creative life, beyond the last written poem.

The arrangement of this book is roughly chronological, although I do not always discuss the poems within collections in their order of appearance. Some of the poems chosen for analysis are the frequently anthologized pieces, and others are less well known but more explicit in their philosophical content. Stevens tended to disparage explicitness—as he does in "Man Carrying Thing"—and to drop from later collections poems in which he believed he had been too direct; these poems, however, can serve as glosses for other poems that are more indirect. "Close reading" is a hazardous endeavor, since the overall perspective the reader has on Stevens may affect even the way he or she construes the ambiguous grammatical constructions. Some would rule out close reading entirely as outmoded or limiting. But to follow the course of Stevens's thought, we need to look intently at the individual poems as well as to locate them in the larger current of his work. It is to be hoped that the overall image produced will highlight a few overlooked poems, widening the circle of what is taken as Stevens's most compelling work.

Reading Stevens is a challenging and invigorating struggle. Developing an addiction to the work may be cause or effect of a deep involvement with modern American poetry, with its embedded fragments of philosophy, history, psychology, and other arts and sciences. I have tried to interpret from a consistent viewpoint so that at least the basis for interpretation is clear. The materials have been arranged in such a way that reading a chapter or a discussion of a group of poems should be useful to those seeking an introduction to a particular work. This way of reading the poems should allow readers who have different theoretical frameworks to use my interpretations as a springboard for their own readings.

Stevens, after all, belongs to all who would claim him. This group has grown immensely, expanding from the initial group of poets who first appreciated his work to include philosophers, priests, physicists, and theorists of all persuasions. Stevens erases boundaries, one of the qualities that makes him so appealing to our time. His inexhaustibility allows each journey to provide new vistas, and I hope that this brief overview will provide another viable perspective.

Acknowledgments

I would like to thank Texas A&M University for supporting my research through the award of a faculty development leave, and the English Department at Texas A&M for allotting me the space and resources to complete my project. I would also like to thank my husband Hugh and my children, Stephanie, Hugh, Paul, and Peter, for being there. A number of my colleagues provided encouragement and help, among them, Robert Boenig, Bedford Clark, Charlene Clark, David Craig, Robert L. Gale, Sylvia Grider, Clinton Machann, Katherine O'Keeffe, and Susan Williams. I am grateful for the help of the members of my graduate class on Wallace Stevens, whose ideas often stimulated mine; the freshness of their approach to Stevens has been a continual excitement. These young scholars include Joy Castro, Kyu-Hyung Cho, Douglas Jordan, Joon-Hwan Kim, and Kenneth Womack. The critics Beverly Coyle and the late Peter Brazeau gave me ideas and information in letters and conversations. The late Holly Stevens also provided materials for my use. Above all, I would like to thank Sister Bernetta Quinn, O.S.F., who has proved to be an invaluable resource throughout this project.

Chronology

1942   *Parts of a World* published by Knopf. *Notes toward a Supreme Fiction* published by Cummington Press in a limited edition.

1945   Elected to the National Institute of Arts and Letters. *Esthétique du Mal* published by Cummington Press in a limited edition.

1947   *Transport to Summer* published by Knopf. Grandson Peter Reed Hanchak born 26 April.

1949   Awarded Bollingen Prize in Poetry.

1950   *The Auroras of Autumn* published by Knopf.

1951   Receives 1950 National Book Award for Poetry. Receives Gold Medal of the Poetry Society of America. *The Necessary Angel: Essays on Reality and the Imagination* published by Knopf.

1953   *Selected Poems* published by Faber and Faber in England.

1954   *The Collected Poems* published by Knopf. *Mattino Domenicale*, Stevens poems translated by Renato Poggioli, published by Giulio Einaudi Editore.

1955   Receives 1954 National Book Award for *The Collected Poems*. Exploratory operation on 26 April results in diagnosis of incurable stomach cancer. Receives Pulitzer Prize for Poetry. Dies 2 August in Hartford.

1957   *Opus Posthumous* published by Knopf.

1963   Elsie Stevens dies 19 February.

1967   *Letters of Wallace Stevens*, edited by Holly Stevens, published by Knopf.

1992   Holly Bright Stevens dies 4 March.

Chapter One

"The Marvelous Sophomore": The Poems of *Harmonium*

The myth of Wallace Stevens is one of physical, intellectual, and poetic largeness. His reality is hard to pin down, a circumstance that would have pleased him. Biographies were slow to appear, perhaps because there is so much trivial information about him and so little that is clear and definitive. A man who lived an intensely inward life, Stevens did little that would make the headlines or even cause much comment. Because the plainly stated facts of his life are relatively uncommunicative, he must be read from his poems. His work, however, generates radically inconsistent images of the man. The presence within the poems is like the shadowy mountain figure of "Chocorua to Its Neighbor"—magical, portentous, elusive. The image in his poems most frequently encountered is of the poet-philosopher-priest of the secular epiphany finding in poetry a substitute for religion.

But how accurate is this image? Certainly much has been made of his persistent application of the terminology of Christianity to the things of this world. Lucy Beckett, Leonora Woodman, and Adelaide Kirby Morris are only a few of the critics who have discussed Stevens's use of religious terms and diction for a secular purpose.[1] Their Stevens appears as a nostalgic modernist who arrives at a deification of the human imagination. The "interior paramour," imagination as value, is the only comfort: "We say that God and the imagination are one . . . / How high that highest candle lights the dark."[2] Only a few critics have examined closely the deep strain of the mystical in Stevens, the desire for transcendence that runs from his first to his last poems and is a part of the impulse in him that made him join the Roman Catholic Church during his last illness. Among those who have, two have produced outstanding readings: Barbara Fisher and Joseph Carroll.[3] They show a different Stevens, one for whom "the plain sense of things" was a beginning rather than an end.

In fact, the poems, essays, and letters support this second view of Stevens. His immersion in the heady intellectual world of Harvard at the turn of the century did not produce an explosive confrontation with the

1

"real world" that resulted in a simple evaporation of his childhood faith. Rather, his encounters with a spectrum of philosophies and poetics encouraged him to try out substitutes for his childhood's solid Protestantism. "The major poetic idea in the world is and always has been the idea of God," he wrote to Henry Church, probably his best friend. "One of the visible movements of the modern imagination is the movement away from the idea of God. The poetry that created the idea of God will either adapt it to our different intelligence, or create a substitute for it, or make it unnecessary. These alternatives probably mean the same thing."[4]

The ambivalence of the reflections in this ambiguous letter, written in 1940 when Stevens was working on the poems of *Parts of a World* (1942), is clear. But his notions of what could be the adaptation of, or the substitute for, the idea of God preoccupied him for the rest of his career. His poetry considers God as change, God as the glorified self, God as a Zen-like presence in absence, and God as imagination—no longer the interior paramour but what he describes in a late poem as the "external master of knowledge."[5] Some of the major figures who inspired Stevens's philosophical quest were William James, Plotinus, Santayana, Dante, Croce, Plato, Nietzsche, Jung—writers for whom forms were often unconventionally invested with sacred meanings. David Jarraway, David La Guardia, Richard Sawaya, and a host of others, in addition to Carroll and Fisher, have examined the individual influence of these thinkers. But in general, those who have looked at Stevens's metaphysical leanings have not gone far enough. The nostalgia for lost truths and the desire for a replacement metaphysic are the motive for the entire work, from *Harmonium* onward.

Stevens's childhood religion was a product of his time and place. On 2 October 1879, Wallace Stevens was born in Reading, Pennsylvania, the second child of a middle-class couple whose belief in the Protestant work ethic was combined with aristocratic behavior and expectations. His father, Garrett Stevens, a lawyer upon whom the need to make a living always weighed heavily, early transferred this burden of responsibility to his son. His mother, Margarethe Catharine Zeller, a woman of faith and imagination and an active church member who read the Bible daily, attempted to pass on her firm belief in Christianity. In his letters and journals, the young Wallace Stevens identified his father with the practical, the need to make a living in the world of men, and his devout mother with the poetic. From the beginnings of his intellectual life, imagination was allied with faith, reality with reason.

The Dutch Reformed Church of Stevens's father, as well as his mother's First Presbyterian Church, presented straightforward, unornamented brands of Christianity. A picture of the church and the pew where Stevens's ancestors worshiped for over 200 years is included in Joan Richardson's biography and reminds many of the tedium of long services and uncompromising sermons, the Sunday morning duty that served as a generous tithe of the children's weekend freedom.[6] As a young man, Stevens rejected the dogma and the duty, and yet he made it clear that he wanted his fiancée, Elsie Moll, to continue to go to church. He wrote her in 1907: "It has always been a particular desire of mine to see you join church. . . . I am very, very glad to know that you are now on the road. —I am not in the least religious" (*LWS*, 96). The desired (and most desirable) image of his beloved in church bears on the division between a logical-practical-masculine side of life and a feeling-artistic-feminine side he then believed in: "I'd rather see you going to church than know that you were as wise as Plato and Haeckel rolled into one, and I'd rather sing some old chestnut out of the hymn-book with you, surrounded by 'stupid' people, than listen to all the wise men in the world" (*LWS*, 96). This letter writer's need for faith is counterbalanced by his need to disclaim it. "He" claims to be "not in the least religious," but "she," his other self, muse and medium, can barely be conceived of without a simple faith. A few years later, however, in "Sunday Morning," a male voice would be telling a reluctant woman to shed her (feminine and Christian) faith and try on his new (masculine and pagan) one.

Stevens's educational goals were at first determined by his father. Beginning in 1897, he attended Harvard for three years, rubbing minds with Irving Babbitt and George Santayana and publishing poems in the *Harvard Advocate*, although he planned to follow his father's goal for him and become a lawyer. While studying law and planning to take the bar exam, he indulged his literary ambitions as a hobby and enjoyed the intellectual experimentation that characterized the university at the turn of the century. It was at Harvard that he acquainted himself with the French poets whose influence can be seen in *Harmonium* and whose mark on his work he acknowledged in a letter to René Taupin with the comment, "La légèreté, la grâce, le son et la couleur du français ont eu sur moi une influence indéniable et une influence précieuse" (The lightness, the grace, the color, and the sound of French have had an undeniable and a precious influence on me). Taupin was particularly struck by Stevens's preciosity and noted that Stevens imported quite a bit of French into his poems.[7] Although Stevens later disclaimed the influence of specific authors or works, he clearly associated France and the French with style and technique, with "the gaiety of language" (*CP*, 322), and sometimes with the feminine. France became one of his symbolic locations, although he never visited the country. In "Explanation," the speaker explains,

> Ach, Mutter, this old black dress,
> I've been embroidering
> French flowers on it. (*CP*, 72)

The French became for Stevens the self-consciously imagined, "embroidered" world, as opposed to the reality of the American scene. Other countries and regions he associated with particular colors, textures, and impressions to produce an interior map that showed a melding of the techniques of the French symbolists and the American realists.

In 1900 Stevens's literary ambitions triumphed temporarily over his father's wishes for him, and he decided in favor of a career as a journalist. He went off to New York, where he worked briefly as a reporter for the *New York Tribune*, as a freelancer, and as an editorial assistant for the monthly magazine *World's Work*. But finding that he was not able to support himself as a journalist, at least not according to his own somewhat patrician standards, he enrolled in New York Law School in 1901 and was admitted to the bar in 1904. That same year, on a visit to Reading, he met the outstandingly beautiful Elsie Moll, who was to be his wife. (She would later be the model for the Liberty Head dime.) Their long engagement was filled with letters outlining the developing poet's theories and impressions. He had by now divided his life neatly in two: the practical side working toward a materially fulfilling life, and the imaginative side, invested in Elsie, playing with ideas and images. Stevens wrote poems for Elsie and presented her with two carefully hand-assembled "June Books" on her birthdays in 1908 and 1909; they contained poems that were typically end-of-the-century in style and content but nevertheless carried the seeds of his lifelong interest in theories of creative perception. Stevens thought of his early poems as "ladylike" (*LWS*, 180), and of poetry writing in general as a ladylike occupation to which he could retreat from the real world of what was at the time the almost exclusively male world of business. During the years of their engagement, they saw each other little. Stevens's few extant letters to Elsie from this period—she destroyed most of them—show her, or at least the imagined Elsie, in the role of muse to the young poet.

Stevens and Elsie Moll were married in 1909, after he had held for a time his position on the legal staff of the American Bonding Company and felt secure enough to take this step. He continued to write, and living in New York gave him access to the currents of innovation that were flowing through the art world just after the turn of the century. In college, he had made the acquaintance of Walter Conrad Arensberg, a wealthy poet and dilettante whose salon in New York became the center for experimental artists such as Marcel Duchamp and Walter Pach and for poets interested in their art. The Armory Show in 1913 dramatically introduced cubism to the American scene. Arensberg was very taken by it, and he would cover the walls of his salon with cubist works.

Stevens spent evenings at the Arensberg salon arguing with advocates of the most avant-garde in art, picking up their concerns and techniques.[8] The electric new movements must have seemed like an energetic antidote to the end-of-the-century genteel lassitude, a vitalizing force that better fit his concept of "masculine" activity; they gave him a justification for seriously pursuing poetry.

In 1916 Stevens joined the Hartford Accident and Indemnity Company—the firm he remained with for the rest of his life—and that year he also moved to Hartford. His first published poems, which show the distinctive influence of his New York friends, appeared in *Trend* in 1914; after that, he published frequently in the small magazines, including *Poetry*, which had been started up by Harriet Monroe in 1912. His first collection, *Harmonium*, was published by Alfred A. Knopf in 1923, bringing the fully developed, highly individualistic poet into the public eye.

The difference between the Stevens of the June Books and the voice of *Harmonium* is overwhelming; it seems inconceivable that the gentle lyricist could have produced such richly ambiguous, multitextured work. Many of the *Harmonium* poems have hard, glittery surfaces; they contain haiku-like nature images, archaisms, foreign phrases, grammatical obscurities, oblique allusions, neologisms, topical references. Yet these elements are not surface ornaments, as they were for some of Stevens's contemporaries, but are integral to his main theme of the loss of faith and the search for a replacement suitable for a changed and decentered world.

A major factor in this change may well have been Stevens's contact with Walter Arensberg's art circle, a collection of experimentalists of every stripe who shared their products and theories. Glen MacLeod has clarified the major role played in Stevens's development by two fluid and overlapping New York groups. The writers Donald Evans, Allen and

Louise Norton, and Carl van Vechten produced *Trend* magazine—the avant-garde literary journal in which Stevens published his first postgraduate poems—and were fin-de-siècle in their search for the new and their scorn of the bourgeois. The Arensberg salon centered on the visual arts and included such people as the experimental artists Charles Demuth, Man Ray, Francis Picabia, and Marcel Duchamp—radical revisionists who were finding form in the formless and meaning in incoherence.

Stevens was swept up by the energy in the art world at the turn of the century; the spirit of revolution was in the wind. Experimental artists and writers were attempting to bring literature and the arts closer together, to perceive words as colors or textures—to make poetry a plastic art. Young writers were attracted to the Dadaists (1916–23), who destroyed traditional forms by comic derision, making chance, intuition, and the irrational the guiding principles of their art. Also persuasive were the futurists in the 1910s and early 1920s, who were in love with the mechanical; their works captured the energy and motion of the machine age. Stevens was also influenced by impressionism and cubism—the former in particular for the way it used specific techniques, such as tiny brush strokes, to capture qualities of light, and the latter for its reductions and distortions. Duchamp especially fascinated Stevens with his fusion of cubism and futurism in "Nude Descending a Staircase," the painting that appalled the bourgeoisie in the 1913 Armory Show, and his still more revolutionary Dadaist art that came later. A particular quirk Stevens identified with in the work was the reification of the human and the anthropomorphism of things and concepts: for both artist and poet, people were replaced by things, and things by people. The Dadaists, like Stevens, wished to wrench out of context, and thereby destroy, established (stale) meanings (MacLeod, 26–27). The effect of these movements was to make violence a significant element of art, an effect that intrigued Stevens. Creating new art from the rubble of the old, which the Dadaists sometimes did literally, may have appealed to Stevens on several levels.

In the *Harmonium* poems, the cosmic ennui and the nostalgia of the aesthetes blend with the experimentation of the artists and writers of the 1910s. Stevens's sense of place develops, geographic locale becoming a tentative locus for the metaphysical. Also appearing in his first work are the initial incarnations of what will develop into the interior paramour, the female doubled self that is mistress and muse, emanation of earth and intimation of divinity. She appears as the woman in "Sunday Morning," the "One of Fictive Music," the Infanta Marina, Susanna of "Peter Quince," and elsewhere; the negatively influential women of "Le

Monocle de Mon Oncle" and "The Comedian as the Letter C" figure into the picture as well. Stevens's notion of woman as the equivalent of faith or belief, as expressed in the letter to his bride-to-be quoted earlier, is interrogated and transformed but never discarded. Stevens brings all the artillery of the new art movements to bear on these old questions. Although it seemed almost from the beginning that Stevens's marriage would not fulfill his hopes, this disappointment only made the muse figure more elusive.

Formally, the poems of *Harmonium* range from the lush, partly rhymed verse of "To One of Fictive Music" through the careful blank verse of "Sunday Morning" to the spare Oriental arrangements of "Thirteen Ways of Looking at a Blackbird." Because the voice is not as yet fully Stevens's own, one can pick out particular influences in the poems. The Orientalism of early Pound can be seen in "Thirteen Ways of Looking at a Blackbird," and the imagist manifesto can be illustrated by "The Public Square." The romantics, Wordsworth especially, are evoked, probably deliberately, in "Sunday Morning."

Harmonium stands out from Stevens's later work owing to the density and concreteness of its images. Each poem has a distinct separateness and flavor; this effect of individuality is underscored by the inconsistency between the poems. They define the problem of the lost metaphysic, returning again and again to this sense of loss, but the proposed substitutes are neither clear nor uniform. Just as Crispin of "The Comedian as the Letter C" conceives his voyaging to be an "Up and down between two elements" (*CP*, 35), so too is Stevens buffeted back and forth as he embraces first one and then the other of two contradictory premises about the relative values of day and night, the masculine and the feminine, the real and the imagined.

"Life is an affair of people not of places," Stevens said in one of his playfully serious "Adagia." "But for me life is an affair of places and that is the trouble" (*OP*, 185). The course of Stevens's work is marked by a movement from the particulars of place to the concept of place in its broadest and most metaphysical sense. In *Harmonium*, the element of local habitation is strong. The poems represent an energetic attempt to penetrate place with the mind, often resulting in the investment of place with femininity: the sunlight becomes a woman, the marina becomes a woman, and so on. A main characteristic of the collection is the merging of the muse with natural forms, the coming together of body and spirit, or "inspiration." The poems evoke manifestations of inspiration and blocks to it, but they do not find clear or satisfying solutions to the problems they present. Even the long, much-discussed "Comedian as the Letter C" backs off from the problem of merging the imagined and the real that Crispin has dealt with for a lifetime. "Le Monocle de Mon Oncle" explores the unbridgeable gap between the imagined and the real but provides no solution besides the pose of ironic detachment.

Indeed, this irony is rampant in *Harmonium*; together with the work's glitter, it prompted the first critical judgment that Stevens was a "dandy."[9] In the poems that express this fin-de-siècle jadedness, however, there is always a distancing from that position: we look through "le monocle de mon oncle," not the poet's naked eye, and from this angle, we see the self-mocking world-weariness of the disappointed aging lover. Already in *Harmonium* Stevens is doing his favorite conjurer's trick, the disappearance of the magician himself into the empty hat. The difficulty of determining which of a Stevens poem's various voices are Stevens himself—the real or "felt" voice—and which are ironic continues to plague interpretation and divide critics. Stevens's two modes, exaltation and irony, often are too close for comfortable distinction.

"Sunday Morning" offers one of Stevens's first substitutes for Christianity: natural religion, or paganism. Stevens said very little about this poem after writing it, other than to note in 1928 that "the poem is simply an expression of paganism" (*LWS*, 250) and later, in 1944, to indicate that Hi Simons was correct in assuming that the poem suggests "a naturalistic religion as a substitute for supernaturalism" (*LWS*, 464). Stevens tended to dismiss questions about or interpretations of this poem. His offhandedness about what remains perhaps his most anthologized work may suggest that he thought the poem's interpretation to be clear and obvious. His dismissiveness may also have implied that the poem's propositions did not preoccupy him further or later. And yet they clearly did: the "Sunday Morning" questions recur in various guises on through the writing of his last work.

One of the more traditional in form of Stevens's poems, "Sunday Morning" consists of blank-verse sections of varying lengths. The poem develops as an argument between two voices: the tentative, questioning tones of the woman, whose enjoyment of the pleasures of this world is cut by the awareness of death, and another, more authoritative voice that seeks to reassure her that the world is enough to satisfy, that in fact it is all the satisfaction there is. A. Walton Litz shows the parallel between the thesis of "Sunday Morning" and William James's comment that "the earth of things, long thrown into shadow by the glories of the upper ether, must resume its rights."[10]

In the first section, the woman is enjoying "complacencies of the peignoir, and late / Coffee and oranges in a sunny chair" (*CP*, 66), but the very enjoyment of life leads her to realize its transience, to remember her church—which she is not attending at the time—and to allow fear and guilt to disturb her pleasure. The second section picks up the argument with the other voice, which asks, "Why should she give her bounty to the dead?" Should not this world provide compensation for the lost heaven? She should embrace her own divinity, the other voice suggests, and let herself be a mirror of the nature that engendered her and of which she is a part. Her emotions are extensions of nature,

> Passions of rain, or moods in falling snow;
> Grievings in loneliness, or unsubdued
> Elations when the forest blooms. . . . (*CP*, 67)

One with nature, she should not try to separate herself from it and redefine herself as something unnatural or supernatural.

The third section takes up the history of divinity, tracing godhead from the totally inhuman Jove through the partly human Jesus to the fully human god suggested by the poem. To invest the human with the divine would make earth into paradise, the sky becoming fully our own rather than a division between earth and heaven. The fourth section returns to the woman's perspective. She is not entirely willing to accept the argument because she realizes that the paradise offered is not permanent. The other voice then assures her that there is a permanence, a permanence of the human, although not of the individual. To her claim in part 5 that she needs individual continuity, the other voice offers the consolation that "Death is the mother of beauty" (*CP*, 69): the cycle of ripening, fruition, and decay causes desire, which would not exist without the realization of transience. The sixth section hypothesizes a static heaven in which the ripe fruit never falls; such a place would be boring, not beautiful. Only change causes beauty, and change entails beginnings and endings; hence, "Death is the mother of beauty."

The alternative to Christianity is suggested in part 7—"a ring of men" chanting "their boisterous devotion to the sun" (*CP*, 70). Human energy should recognize the source of nature's energy as kin; this recognition would reestablish the participation of humans in nature, which is not so much mystical as actual. This argument is presented as a conclusive one, and the woman accepts it. Her recognition that Jesus is a historical figure and that she is alone, a part of "unsponsored" nature, frees her from the prison in which her traditional beliefs had locked her. The conclusion, a merging of the woman's perception with that of the other voice, is a Wordsworth-like picture of the sweet earth, with overtones of an elegy for the notion of personal immortality. The joined voices proclaim that we are no different from the "casual flocks of pigeons" (*CP*, 70) whose flight is not patterned but casual, and whose indecipherable movements or "ambiguous undulations" (*CP*, 70) are nevertheless a form of untranslatable language, a kind of inscription or self-definition that is natural rather than superimposed. Stevens's later work is preoccupied with the notion that true order must be found in nature rather than forced on it, but he later finds orders different from the simple natural rhythms.

This poem uses the figure of the woman to work through the objections to the discarding of Christianity. Stevens himself is both the woman and her opponent. "Sunday Morning" is the first full presentation of Stevens's lifelong central motif, the search for a sustaining fiction. But the answers he provides are clearly problematic to him as well as to the reader. Parts 7 and 8 both seem to be conclusions, but they do not cohere. "Boisterous devotion" characterizes part 7: the reborn pagan males seek to merge with the life source, yielding their individuality to its larger identity. Part 8, however, is muted. The lushness of nature affords no *participation mystique* but rather suggests isolation and separation. The freedom the woman has won by relinquishing her Christian faith provides no real compensation except a sense of the vulnerability of all nature. Stevens allowed Harriet Monroe to publish the poem with part 7 last, embedding part 8 earlier in the narrative (*LWS*, 183–84). It would seem that he did not know exactly where he wanted the poem to go or how seriously he wanted the paganism to be taken. Paganism does offer a form of transcendence, whereas simple identification with the natural cycles does not. His choice of elegy over energy seems to negate the scene of the sun worshipers, which then appears artificial and contrived in contrast with the poem's ending. As Carroll points out, "despite its apparent persuasiveness, its implicit claim to have solved the problem it poses is premature."[11]

The same problem appears in a more condensed form in "The Emperor of Ice-Cream," whose conclusion is equally unsatisfying. The frequently anthologized poem that Stevens once claimed was his favorite brings the creative forces face to face with their negation. The poem's matter-of-fact tone undercuts itself, providing a perfect vehicle for a proclamation of surface as substance. There are two presences in the poem, the representatives of ordinary, everyday life, and the woman, who represents ordinary death. The poem is neatly cut in two. In the first section, it seems that a party is being prepared: the "muscular" cigar-roller is asked to whip up "concupiscent curds," ice cream. The "wenches" are loitering about, and the boys are asked to "bring flowers in last month's newspapers"—nothing is so dead as yesterday's news, useful only as wrappings to be thrown away. The scene suggests celebration; in fact, this is a party with a strong sexual element. But what is being commemorated is a dead woman, described in the second half of the poem. The dead woman was poor—she had a dresser made of cheap wood, with missing glass knobs—yet she tried to make her life more colorful by embroidering birds on her white sheets. Still, now she is dead: this fact must be recognized, not glossed over. What seems to be, is. The appearance of a thing is its substance. "Let be be finale of seem." The only thing to celebrate is flux—"The only emperor is the emperor of ice-cream" (*CP*, 64).

The images in the poem combine to give a stereoscopic view of life-in-death and death-in-life: flowers wrapped in old news, embroidered sheets turned into shrouds. This poem's insistence upon the finality of death and its repeated cry that death's finality is a good echoes throughout *Harmonium*. That it is their melting that makes sensuous joys delightful, that stasis can provide only boredom whereas change brings delight, are themes that are repeated until the celebration of change becomes frenetic. The reader is not convinced. The writer may have been to some extent: the poem remained among Stevens's favorites for its expression of "something of the essential gaudiness of poetry" (*LWS*, 263). Typical of Stevens's early attempts to replace the lost metaphysic is this substitution of temporary style for permanence, this claim that the fact of transience in itself conveys value.

"Peter Quince at the Clavier" is another poem of male and female— this time, Susanna and Peter Quince are elements of the poet—that seems to recommend a form of paganism, in this case implicitly. Traditionally, the poem is seen as a reinterpretation of the notion of art's permanence, an inversion of cliché. Peter Quince, as the director of the naive troupe of tradesmen-players in *Midsummer Night's Dream*, is a comic figure, another of Stevens's comedians; the title gives us the ironic image of Peter Quince at the delicate instrument, his rough hands attempting perhaps a sonata. (Several critics have suggested that the poem imitates the sonata form.) The somewhat awkward would-be lover at his instrument wishes to find some adequate chords to communicate his desire, which he compares to the lust of the elders in the story of Susanna, whose tale is told in those later additions to the book of Daniel that are collected in the biblical *Apocrypha*.[12] Peter Quince suggests that desire is the origin of art; beauty plays on the spirit of the perceiver just as the perceiver plays on the keys of his instrument. There is a correspondence between the dynamic of arousal and that of artistry.

> Just as my fingers on these keys
> Make music, so the selfsame sounds
> On my spirit make a music, too. (*CP*, 89)

The poem develops the theme that "music is feeling" by combining the poetic devices of alliteration, assonance, and consonance with puns on musical terms to suggest the sounds of the musical instruments mentioned, as in this passage describing the feelings of the lascivious elders:

> The basses of their beings throb
> In witching chords, and their thin blood
> Pulse pizzicati of Hosanna. (*CP*, 90)

"Basses" fuses "base," suggesting both "low and unworthy" and "foundation," with the musical term "bass." Musical tone then becomes moral tone. The line "Pulse pizzicati of Hosanna" mimics the plucking of strings but also may suggest the sexual itch. This turning of music into words, and words into music, continues throughout the poem, becoming metaphor as well as genuine verbal music.

In the *Apocrypha*, Susanna is a beautiful and chaste young wife desired by the elders of the church, who tell her that if she will not grant them her favors, they will claim to have witnessed her committing adultery. She refuses, and they accuse her; she is sentenced to death, but God hears her prayers and arranges for Daniel to acquit her by cleverly trapping the elders into giving conflicting narratives. As he usually does, Stevens uses only those elements of the story that fit into his plan. The poet-pianist-player's desire transcends that of the elders. He cannot possess his beloved physically, but he can hold her in his mind in a platonic and permanent sense. Susanna is moved from the world of facts to the world of forms, where her beauty continues to exist.[13]

B. J. Leggett, however, has pointed out that the problems of this poem have not been resolved by commentators. They have not dealt with the fact that Stevens's Susanna is not the innocent wife of the

Apocrypha but a sensual, even lusty virgin; nor have they addressed the abrupt gaps in tone and logic within and between parts of the poem.[14] Using Nietzsche's distinction between Appollonian and Dionysian as intertext, Leggett pulls the poem together as a meditation on the question: "How does the lyric speaker's own subjective feeling, *his* desire, transcend the merely personal, the individual?" (Leggett, 67). The poem's answer is that through the power of music he "surrenders his subjectivity to the Dionysian process" (70), a surrender that happens to Peter Quince and in a sense to Susanna herself. Leggett's interpretation brings the various elements of the poem into balance: the elders, the evocative/provocative Susanna, and Peter Quince all have self-consistent roles in this parable of the creation of lyric poetry through the dissolution of the self in music—through, in fact, a Dionysian ecstasy. Thus, another form of paganism appears, deeper and more sophisticated than the "natural religion" Stevens identifies as belonging to "Sunday Morning." "Peter Quince" shows an effort to find transcendence by elevating the artist to the stature of a god, allowing him to break out of the limitations of self in his creative frenzy. Ultimately, the idea of the loss of self through the transformative process will not "suffice" either but will prove one of a series of efforts to find transcendence.

The two longest poems in *Harmonium*, "Le Monocle de Mon Oncle" and "The Comedian as the Letter C," begin and end in the world of matter. They contribute to Stevens's exploration of the spiritual dimension by showing that, without it, no source is present from which the artist may draw. "Le Monocle" is a long reflective poem that extends disappointment in sex to disappointment in the material world, reaching conclusions far different from those of "Sunday Morning." In discussing this poem, Joseph Carroll cites George Santayana's *Interpretations of Poetry and Religion* (1900), which identifies sex as the wellspring of imaginative life: "For man all nature is a secondary object of sexual passion." Thus, the diminishing of sexual drive would result in a decline of creativity (Carroll, 41). The poem argues with this position, as Stevens once argued one of Santayana's positions with him in an exchange of sonnets.

The series of 12 eleven-line iambic pentameter stanzas begins with a lover's quarrel and a lover's disappointment, contrasted with remembered passion. The disappointment widens to all nature: "No spring can follow past meridian." The "you" addressed in the poem, the wife-lover, wants to affirm a permanence, "a starry connaissance" (*CP*, 13). The speaker will have none of it. He is obsessed with and overwhelmed by the fact of his aging, by his constant awareness of the ripeness and rot cycle, and by the difference he feels between past expectations and present realities. His new sad knowledge is compared to the fall from innocence in the Garden of Eden. His announcement that "No spring can follow past meridian" indicates that no identification with the natural cycle like that of "Sunday Morning" appeals to him. What saddens the speaker most is not only that the flesh is impermanent and sexual pleasure passes and diminishes, but that desire remains, with no attainable object. The woman he addresses has failed him as sexual partner and (therefore?) as muse. Youth and romantic love—the erotic are inextricably bound, and there is no escape from this natural law. Awareness of this situation itself saps creative as well as sexual energy. It would seem from this section that Santayana was right.

The speaker does, however, posit a permanence to oppose to the "starry connaissance" he rejects. He proclaims, "There is a substance in us that prevails" (*CP*, 15). This "substance" seems to be a kind of blank, like the Snow Man's landscape: Carroll describes the "basic slate" as "a substratum of experience" that is "featureless, beyond change, and . . . thus impervious to the decline of sexual verve" (44). Thus, there is still something on which the older poet can draw for creativity. If the erotic evaporates, there remains the desire for the metaphysical, which also disappoints.

The shift to metaphysical longing comes abruptly, without transition:

> The mules that angels ride come slowly down
> The blazing passes, from beyond the sun. . . .
> Meantime, centurions guffaw and beat
> Their shrilling tankards on the table-boards.
> This parable, in sense, amounts to this:
> The honey of heaven may or may not come,
> But that of earth both comes and goes at once.
> Suppose these couriers brought amid their train
> A damsel heightened by eternal bloom. (*CP*, 15)

Stevens glosses the last few lines in a letter, commenting, "But would the honey of heaven be so uncertain if the mules that angels ride brought a damsel heightened by eternal bloom, that is to say, brought a specifically divine revelation, not merely angelic transformation of ourselves? The trouble with the idea of heaven is that it is merely an idea of the earth" (*LWS*, 464). It may be relevant to consider the sexual implications of the "honey of heaven" line, in connection with the mysterious tree of part 10 that

> . . . stands gigantic, with a certain tip
> To which all birds come sometime in their time.
> But when they go that tip still tips the tree. (*CP*, 17)

The tree may be a representation of a kind of phallicism that is a general drive, the earth's male verve. The only permanence is this abstract life force, the force of creativeness in which individuals partake briefly. But desire, even without object, remains.

> If sex were all, then every trembling hand
> Could make us squeak, like dolls, the wished-for words,
> But note the unconscionable treachery of fate,
> That makes us weep, laugh, grunt and groan, and shout
> Doleful heroics, pinching gestures forth
> From madness or delight, without regard
> To that first, foremost law. Anguishing hour! (*CP*, 17)

Desire for the unattainable can only be mocked by all the signs of earth's plenty.

"Mon Oncle" provides and then glosses one metaphor after another, explaining pedantically that this is what it is doing. Yet the last metaphor, the blue and white pigeons and the dark and rose rabbis, remains unglossed and obscure. The pigeons of youth and age are clear enough, but the two rabbis both seem to represent phases of youth in which innocence studies nature from a state of natural sympathy, before the maturing observer learned "that fluttering things had so distinct a shade." The recognition of the shade of fluttering things is a realization of the limits of that which—like sexual verve—seemed unlimited. Moreover, the conclusion of this poem is much like that of "Sunday Morning," with its pigeons that glide "downward to darkness on extended wings" (*CP*, 18). "Mon Oncle," then, posits no natural religion. It offers the alternatives of revelation (as unlikely as angels riding mules down from heaven) or resignation to diminishment and annihilation. The old scholar of love looks for a new, transcendent definition of it but does not find it. He remains suspended between fleshly and spiritual longings, resigned and ironical.

The other long poem, "The Comedian as the Letter C," does not provide a more favorable solution for the artist, although it may do so for the lover. Joseph Carroll explicates "Comedian" as "a parable of a doctrinal course that leads away from the writing of poetry" (36), pointing out that "the hypotheses that govern the course of Crispin's adventure comprehend the full range of doctrinal alternatives available to Stevens in his early poetry" (*CP*, 36). The proposition "Man is the intelligence of his soil" is revised by Crispin's experience to "His soil is man's intelligence" (*CP*, 36); Carroll explains that these two propositions are parallel to Emerson's distinction between the idealist and the materialist: "In the order of thought, the materialist takes his departure from the external world, and esteems man as one product of that. The idealist takes his departure from his consciousness, and reckons the world an appearance."[15] Crispin slips from the world of the idealist to the materialist's world of substance (Carroll, 57) but finds that the world of the "soil" is as barren imaginatively as it is fruitful physically. In the process, Crispin goes through a series of discoveries, each of which transports him into a new imaginative realm. But each discovery proves unsatisfying and must be discarded. In commenting on the poem, Stevens said, "I suppose that the way of all mind is from romanticism to realism, to fatalism and then to indifferentism, unless the cycle re-commences and the thing goes from indifferentism back to romanticism all over again" (*LWS*, 350). In the poem, the process does not repeat itself; it stops. In this commentary, written long after he was at work on other projects, Stevens goes on to say that "what the world looks forward to is a new romanticism, a new belief" (*LWS*, 350). At the time of the later reflection, Stevens had abandoned the practical garden and gone back to search for a less materialistic solution.

"The Comedian as the Letter C" takes Stevens's pursuit of the real as far as it will go in the direction of the world of fact. By far the longest poem in *Harmonium*, "Comedian" is a blank-verse exploration of poetics, a narrative of an educational process that ends in a stalemate. Crispin is a valet; Le Sage's Crispin was a foolish valet. Saint Crispin was a traveler. He and his brother Crispinius, the patron saints of shoemakers, left the shelter of their noble Roman family to traipse around France making converts (and shoes). Stevens's maternal grandfather was a shoemaker, a fact in which Stevens took pride (Richardson I, 40).

Stevens commented that one of his poem's aims was to represent "the sounds of the letter C"; in Stevens's Larousse French dictionary, the section of words beginning with *C* would have been heralded by the figure of a comic jester juggling symbols of other *C* words.[16] Yet Crispin is not to be too lightly dismissed; he is the comic hero of a world that must be a cosmic comedy, not unlike the cosmos envisioned in "A High-Toned Old Christian Woman." The poet-hero of the cosmic comedy must be a practical man, not a dark, romantic cloud-strider. Stevens himself does not dismiss Crispin but returns to him in later poems.

The first section, "The World without Imagination," takes Crispin through the first proposition: ". . . man is the intelligence of his soil, / The sovereign ghost" (*CP*, 27). Initially, Crispin is a romantic who places himself at the center of his universe as maker and namer. He is the "Socrates / of snails," *principium* (base) and *lex* (law). On the sea, Crispin can no longer believe in this arrangement. Wrenched away from the relatively controllable and complaisant land, he cannot factor the vast experience of the sea into his limited system. First he projects his land-locked fantasies on to the new shifting medium: his "barber's eye" sees the waves as "mustachios." But he is unable to control this environment; the result is that "Crispin was washed away by magnitude," his identity dissolved. This is the Crispin whose characteristic was "verboseness," who carries the freight of his standard-issue associations—the end-of-the-century man. He is "annulled." The sea dissolves its god, Triton, and also the valet Crispin—the strong experience a stripping of meaning.

> . . . nothing of himself
> Remained, except some starker, barer self
> In a starker, barer world. (*CP*, 27)

His first experiences have stripped away the old romantic, leaving him ready for renewal.

The new Crispin is a realist, but he is trapped by his realism. If he is unable to "evade / In poems of plums, the strict austerity / Of one vast subjugating, final tone" (*CP*, 30), then he is brought to the edge of the minimum—instead of freedom from the past, he is bound to the present, for he cannot evade the fact that every addition to the real is in fact a subtraction, a diminution of its realness. "Concerning the Thunderstorms of Yucatan" traces the attempt on Crispin's part to create an aesthetic appropriate to the new world he is encountering. In the tropical world of violent and exotic color and sound, he tries to celebrate the "savagery of palms," creating a new aesthetic of the "moonlight on the thick, cadaverous bloom / That yuccas breed" and the "panther's tread" (*CP*, 31). But this new poetic, composed as it is of "the fabulous and its intrinsic verse," is also unsatisfactory. There is too much self-indulgence, too much rolling in the senses. This aesthetic is one form of naturalism—a study of the barbaric—that Crispin must discard. The earth has grown "too juicily opulent" (*CP*, 32). Crispin must reject the overly fecund world, as the speaker will in "Farewell to Florida," the first poem in the second collection.

A storm having driven Crispin to seek sanctuary in the cathedral, he has a new aesthetic experience, which might be described as the experience of pure meditation. Now

> . . . his mind was free
> And more than free, elate, intent, profound
> And studious of a self possessing him. (*CP*, 33)

He is listening now to himself, to the world, instead of attempting to project his preconceptions on it. But this too is only a passage, through which he will progress to other stages. The world of pure reflection is finally no more satisfying than the world of pure matter. Moonlight misleads. Uncontrolled by any reality, it provides illusion.

"Approaching Carolina" leads Crispin further into the naturalist phase, on the way to which he becomes more and more aware of what is happening to him and why he is unable to get a fix on the world and so describe it. He is now "fagot in the lunar fire"—fire of the imagination—and desires to bring about union with the world, "relentless contact." Because of this unfulfillable desire, he has denied himself "many poems": they would be only about appearances, "sea-masks," not about the real. He is paralyzed again by the sense that any creation is a falsification, and the moonlight that might give him a "liaison" with his environment was a will-o'-the-wisp, a misleading light.

> . . . it seemed
> Illusive, faint, more mist than moon, perverse
> Wrong as a divigation to Peking. (*CP*, 34)

He then concludes that his progress is a sort of dialectic, his voyage "an up and down between two elements, / A fluctuating between sun and moon," and then the return to "the indulgences / That in the moonlight have their habitude" (*CP*, 35).

Nevertheless, if moonlight is too romantic for him, "a passionately niggling nightingale," and if sunlight is too strong, Crispin still searches for a realistic aesthetic appropriate to the new world. On the Carolina shore, he seems to find one, the stink of the ordinary:

> He savored rankness like a sensualist.
> He marked the marshy ground around the dock,
> The crawling railroad spur, the rotten fence,
> Curriculum for the marvelous sophomore. (*CP*, 36)

Now he turns to the "essential prose" as the one source for his poetry, but from this point he begins to play with the idea of a new romanticism, which is explored in "The Idea of a Colony."

  This section begins with a revision of the poem's first proposition, which, as Joseph Carroll rightly points out, is the turning point of the poem. "Nota: his soil is man's intelligence. / That's better. That's worth crossing seas to find." Human beings do not define their environment, but it defines them. That realized, Crispin begins to plan a systematized poetic of this truth, a colony in which each environment produces its own appropriate spokespersons:

> The man in Georgia waking among pines
> Should be pine-spokesman. . . .
> Sepulchral senors, bibbling pale mescal,
> Should make the intricate Sierra scan. (*CP*, 38)

But to systematize is to falsify, and reviewing his plans, Crispin realizes that the plans themselves were romantic and "Contained in their afflatus the reproach / That first drove Crispin to his wandering." All dreams are things of moonlight, "let them be expunged." Rather, "Let the rabbit run, the cock declaim." It would seem that the regions themselves must be their own text—the very presence of the interpreter is a false note. Nature is complete without him.

> Trinket pasticcio, flaunting skyey sheets,
> With Crispin as the tiptoe cozener?
> No, no: veracious page on page, exact. (*CP*, 40)

  "A Nice Shady Home" shows Crispin's abandonment of the plan, his "slow recess / To things within his actual eye." He now is a fatalist, accepting the only emperor as the actual, the "plum" that "survives its poems." The substitution of the prose of reality for the poetry of the imaginative life has taken place, and there is nowhere left for Crispin to go except to Stevens's last phase of indifferentism. The last two sections, "A Nice Shady Home" and "And Daughters with Curls," plot the course of Crispin's defeat, his Candide-like withdrawal to his ordinary garden. It is simple contentment that finally defeats Crispin, it would seem:

> . . . if discontent
> Had kept him still the prickling realist . . .
>   . . . he might have come
> To colonize his polar planterdom. (*CP*, 40)

He chooses, however, to live in the actual, the everyday, "So Crispin hasped on the surviving form / For him, of shall or ought to be in is" (*CP*, 40). The line suggests a similar Stevens proposition, "Let be be finale of seem," but it suggests the opposite emotional reaction to this proposition. Instead of jubilance, the joy in change suggested by "concupiscent curds," Crispin's position is one of resignation. He has permitted the soil to become his intelligence and to determine his destiny.

Having done this, the last option is for him to bewail his loss, "Scrawl a tragedian's lament." But he is now an ordinary man. He has found neither a new romanticism nor even a recapitulation of the old one. He accepts that the pleasures of the senses are all he is going to get, and that even those must be won through hard work. His "prismy blonde," the pleasures of bedroom and garden, are the only rewards of his search. The energy that he had wished to put into creative energy goes into these things. The last section describes in detail the four daughters who result from his union with "the prismy blonde"; Frank Kermode claims that the daughters are the seasons, and the descriptions may be read to suggest autumn, winter, spring, and summer.[17] If they are the seasons, they suggest Crispin's submission to the natural cycle of which he is part. But they are also daughters, and his reproduction in kind gives the death blow to any other kind of creation. They leave "no room upon his cloudy knee / Prophetic joint, for its diviner young" (*CP*, 43). Crispin accepts his limits, gobbles down the "turnip" of the world, which turns out to be "the same insoluble lump" he began with. The poem concludes with the suggestion that if Crispin were a comic figure, diminished rather than enlarged by his experiences, it would not matter, since "The relation comes, benignly, to its end . . . / So may the relation of each man be clipped" (*CP*, 46). Thus, the indifferentism has passed from Crispin to the narrator.

Ironically, if we see Stevens as projecting himself into Crispin (and there was in fact a long hiatus between Stevens's writing of *Harmonium* and his next collection, a period that coincided with his daughter Holly's childhood), then the poem becomes a successful example of what it suggests cannot be done. From the beginning to the end of his life, Stevens put on the mask of the clown from time to time, and it is important to remember that Stevens perceived the poem as primarily comic. He had only one objection to the long explication written by Hi Simons in 1939 (aside from a minor cavil over Simons placing him firmly "on the right" politically—a position he ended up accepting in substance). Stevens was concerned that Simons made no mention of the "sounds of the letter C," which are a major part of the poem, intended to accompany Crispin along his journey. The "clipping" of the poem by the last hard *C* provides a phonetically appropriate closure. Stevens stressed that the repeated *C*s produce a comic effect, underscoring the secular-comedy aspect of Crispin's travels through the world (*LWS*, 351). Stevens did not wish for the cosmic comedy to be lost, nor for sound to be entirely lost to sense.

Nevertheless, the comedy cannot obscure the fact that the road Crispin chooses leads nowhere artistically; whether the poem is Stevens's premature farewell to his art is less significant than the fact that the poem is a purging of the transcendent. At each step, as soon as anything more than bare fact slips into the poem, it must be rejected. In a sense, Crispin is the opposite of Bunyan's Christian: he is looking for a paradise or holy city by the elimination of anything that is nonmaterial. And his logical point of arrival is a strictly material paradise. For Voltaire, Candide's garden of mutual effort and daily concern may have been the only compromise, but Stevens is neither Voltaire nor Candide. Submission to the world of fact is loss of possibility. It may be what happens, but it cannot be seen as a good—hence the quirky, shoulder-shrugging conclusion.

By and large, Stevens's shorter *Harmonium* poems tend to represent the world as a secular comedy in which human imagination and ingenuity are pitted against boredom and emptiness and the obscure object of desire is a female spirit of place. Human disappointments, which involve unmet expectations and failures of desire, failures of the nature-goddess-woman to grant favors or even to show up, are presented quasi or outright comically, while desire itself, transmuted into the restless imagination, is exalted. In "Disillusionment of Ten O'Clock," the speaker is sorry that only the standard ghosts, "white night-gowns," haunt the houses; no powerful imagination of the time is about to think of ghosts in "beaded ceintures" or other eighteenth-century trappings. Only those outside of society, such as the old sailor, "drunk and asleep in his boots," live vitally; he "catches tigers / in red weather" (*CP*, 66). It is a vapid society in which sleep and waking life are reversed and decisive action and passionate colors do not exist in the conscious world. In "Depression before Spring," the poet seems to be in love with his elaborate metaphor:

> The hair of my blonde
> Is dazzling,
> As the spittle of cows
> Threading the wind.

Still, despite his promiscuous rhapsodizing, the goddess of nature does not answer his bright call, and "no queen comes / In slipper green" (*CP*, 63). He can approach nature with his creative perceptions, but there is no response; nature remains inscrutably alien. Imagination's unaided attempts fail.

A more elaborate working of the subject of the imagination as escape, here clearly ironic, is "The Ordinary Women," which demonstrates the hazard of uninformed imagining. The women of the title leave their "dry catarrhs" for "guitars," but their trip into the palace of the imagination is fruitless. They are unprepared for the sights that confront them, and when they lean and look at "the canting curlicues / Of heaven and the heavenly script," they read only "of marriage-bed" (*CP*, 10–12). They are unable to escape from the "poverty" that is their natural climate; it is their choice to return to the catarrhs from the "dry guitars" that have been substituted. This poem is unusual in that the would-be artists are women. The theme of disappointment is a leitmotiv throughout *Harmonium*. The speaker claims that the female muse of Florida is too unselective of her disclosures in "O Florida, Venereal Soil." Unable to choose among her many rich possibilities, she offers "the dreadful sundry of this world," instead of revealing—as she should—"A hand that bears a thick-leaved fruit, / A pungent bloom against your shade" (*CP*, 47). Indulgence in the romantic is no panacea, however. The evening star in "Homunculus et la Belle Etoile" is a good light only for those afloat in feelings, "drunkards, poets, widows, / And ladies soon to be married" (*CP*, 25). The romantic is a good tranquilizer, but it does not test the spirit. The moon, a more traditional symbol of the imagination, is "the mother of pathos and pity" in "Lunar Paraphrase" (*CP*, 107). Neither the day world nor the lunar landscape provides true fulfillment. Florida and the tropics attract and repel. The southern fruit is lush and delectable but turns out to be "too juicily opulent" after all.

Those poems more affirmative in their message, at least as far as the artist's potency is concerned, tend to combine the notion of creativity as decreation with the new art techniques, which involve the violent wrenching of old forms to create new ones. The poet seems to flirt with Florida but to be more likely to embrace the Snow Man, whose imagination strips rather than embroiders reality to reach a wintry truth. The coldness of the Snow Man's perception strips the human interpretations from what he sees: because he has "been cold a long time," he can "behold the junipers shagged with ice" and not read any human meanings into the scene that confronts him. The reward for having "a mind of

winter" is to see "nothing that is not there and the nothing that is"—a
perception cleansed of accretions so that it is an awakening or break-
through to reality (*CP*, 10). Other *Harmonium* poems explore the shifting
or fractured perspectives represented in cubist and futurist art. These
poems may nod in the direction of Pound's Orientalism, or they may be
frankly impressionistic. Some of Stevens's poems represent a group of
different perspectives as a panorama, so that the reader gets the effect of
a composite image. Many explore the theory of changing perspectives
and the meaning of observation. Some use shifting perspectives as a
device or a subject: for example, "Metaphors of a Magnifico," "Thirteen
Ways of Looking at a Blackbird," "Sea Surface Full of Clouds." His next
collection continues this practice with poem sequences such as the two
"Botanist on Alp" poems and the two nudity poems. Though these
works are different in many ways, they are held together by the notion
that shifting perspectives form the essential core of art; they affirm style
as substance.

In *Harmonium*, demonstrations of thematic and imagistic complexity,
on the one hand, such as "Thirteen Ways of Looking at a Blackbird,"
alternate with formal poems, such as "To One of Fictive Music," that
express nostalgia for lost faith and evoke a slippery muse, on the other.
Those who would find a unity in Stevens's early work, a seamless fabric
of mind and world, work and poetry, must look hard. The incompatibility of the premises as well as the practices in the *Harmonium* poems suggests that at this time Stevens was indeed "voyaging / Up and down
between two elements." (His ventures into moonland, his "divigation to
Peking," can be examined also by looking at the three very precious
plays he wrote during this period, plays that owe a lot to Noh drama.)[18]
His later work loses this frantic inventiveness as it attempts to get outside the struggle between mind and world so as to achieve another perspective. As it proceeds through the seasons represented by the titles of
some of the later collections, his work becomes phenomenological and
finally mystical, developing a complex aesthetic that either bridges or
transcends opposites.

Chapter Two

"Ghostlier Demarcations":
Ideas of Order

Ideas of Order did not appear until 12 years after *Harmonium*. In the interim, Stevens published only a handful of poems. For a period of five years (1923–28), he wrote next to nothing. The few poems from these years that remained in manuscript or appeared in periodicals express bitterness, resignation, withdrawal, and wry distaste for an antipoetic world that drains energy while giving the lie to myth. Even their names suggest this negativity: "The Shape of the Coroner," "This Vast Inelegance," "Saturday Night at the Chiropodist's," "Metropolitan Melancholy." Stevens's long silence has been variously attributed to the mixed reviews his first collection received, the birth of his daughter Holly in 1924, the necessity of making a living, and marital disappointment. James Longenbach argues convincingly that economic concerns and creative ways of dealing with them were paramount for Stevens during the period of his silence.[1] At least part of the reason for Stevens's diminished output, however, may have been simply his arrival at the end of his logic. His old scenes were written out. The products of the imagination had come to seem too obviously imagined, artificial. He needed to get down to the bedrock of fact.

Biographies with introductory chronologies tend to suggest that nothing much happened to Stevens during these years except for the birth of his daughter; he moved to his home on Westerly Terrace in 1932, and he was named a vice-president of his company in 1934,[2] by which time, however, he was at work on the poems of *Ideas of Order* (1935). In fact, during these silent years, he was fully occupied both at home and at work. He watched over the rearing of Holly, the beautiful baby who would become rotund and large-featured to resemble her father. He and Elsie set the pattern of their life together as partners in maintaining their mutual home and family, but as a couple there was little intimacy between them. They would eventually occupy separate suites at Westerly Terrace. Stevens watched Elsie change and fade—her diminution had already been noted in "Le Monocle de Mon Oncle." It is a shock to the researcher going through the photos of the Stevens family in the Huntington Library to see how quickly the lovely woman of the earliest photos lost her luster—apparently deliberately, for her dowdy clothes were neither fashionable nor fitting. Richardson comments, "Within a few years, the robust beauty of her Liberty head presence had withered into wizened eccentricity, and she dressed like a maiden schoolmarm of sixty."[3]

Stevens's earliest letters to Elsie reveal a desire to enclose himself with her in a magical and exclusive environment. His chosen life pattern did in fact withdraw his family from the world, but he must have keenly felt the difference between the dream and the reality. It is certainly no accident that Candide-figures appear in his poems—the most notable being Crispin—for the story of the quest for the ideal woman who turns out to be unlovely when possessed must have struck a chord. Yet as he had idealized Elsie as muse, he would later construct a myth of the family ironically different from the real one at Westerly Terrace; it would serve as a model of what could or should have been.

At the Hartford, he not only made steady and rapid progress toward his vice-presidency but also found in his chosen career an opportunity to indulge the need for friendship and even beauty that he was unable to satisfy in his family life. He had begun his business trips south right after he joined the Hartford, but in the early 1920s he began making them with Judge Arthur Powell, a business acquaintance who became a fast friend. In 1922 Stevens stayed with Powell at the Long Key Fishing Camp, a luxurious sports resort, and they had such a good time that Stevens began to make regular business trips with Powell to Florida (Brazeau, 97). For the next 20 years, these trips became an escape from his somewhat Puritanical home, for once in Florida he could not only enjoy the lush tropical scenery (about which he wrote home in detail) but the laid-back alcoholic atmosphere (about which he did not). He wrote to a friend after the first trip, on which he was adopted by a group of ebullient Atlanta businessmen:

> I was christened a charter member of the Long Key Fishing Club of Atlanta. The christening occupied about three days, and required just two cases of Scotch. When I traveled home, I was not able to tell whether I was traveling on a sound or a smell. As I remember it, it was very much like a cloud full of Cuban senoritas, cocoanut [*sic*] palms, and waiters carrying ice-water. Since my return I have not cared much for literature. The southerners are a great people. (Brazeau, 97)

Heavy drinking was one way Stevens occasionally escaped from the boredom and frustration of everyday life, and it may have been in these years one of his replacements for poetry. Still, he thought of the silent years as years of advancement and consolidation on the career front. Years later, he wrote to Ronald Lane Latimer, who was being forced by financial pressures to shut down his beloved Alcestis Press, and advised him to accept a difficult situation, as he himself had:

> Giving up The Alcestis Press must be to you what giving up any idea of writing poetry would be to me. Nevertheless, a good many years ago, when I really was a poet in the sense that I was all imagination, and so on, I deliberately gave up writing poetry because, much as I loved it, there were too many other things I wanted not to make an effort to have them. I wanted to do everything that one wants to do at that age: live in a village in France, in a hut in Morocco, or in a piano box at Key West. But I didn't like the idea of being bedeviled all the time about money and I didn't for a moment like the idea of poverty, so I went to work like anybody else and kept at it for a good many years.
>   If you could do that sort of thing, it would not mean anything more than turning away temporarily. (*LWS*, 320)

Duty first, beauty second: thus had Stevens ordered his life, following his father's advice.

For whatever combination of reasons, Stevens spent a long period following the publication of *Harmonium* almost entirely immersed in the world of fact, with the brief Florida fugues his only escape. His attitude toward what he was doing was determined and relatively humorless, compared with the high-hearted clowning of some of his earlier letters and poems. During this time, he wrote relatively few personal letters, and even those tended to be concerned with matters of fact. Many of them spoke of the exigencies of fatherhood in a fatalistic tone, as though Crispin were explaining to a distant, concerned relative his failure to found a colony. Religion clearly preoccupied him still, his ambivalence showing through in all his comments. Two passages in letters to Elsie a week apart in February 1923 show his not quite successful attempts to dismiss religion: "During my walk this morning I dropped into every big church that I passed so that I can honestly say that I went to church most assiduously" (*LWS*, 235). The tone of mockery is at odds with the activity itself. A week later, he talked about the prevalence of "Jesus Saves" signs and their role in southern life, concluding, "I can well imagine how, if I lived in one of the smaller communities a little nearer to the coast, faced constantly by the poverty around me there and feeling acutely the despair that the land and the people are bound to create, I might well depend on some such potent illusion as 'The eternal God is thy refuge'" (*LWS*, 236–37). The unstated corollary seems to be that feeling neither poverty nor despair himself, he had no need for such illusions.

During the period of silence, and then during the gathering momentum of Stevens's reinvolvement with poetry, the letters and poems themselves indicate that Stevens was rejecting all previously held visions of the divine, Christian or pagan, and arriving at a position of unrelieved materialism. In explicating lines 1–4 in part 5 of "The Man with the Blue Guitar," Stevens explains, "Here is the right paraphrase. We live in a world plainly plain. Everything is as you see it. There is no other world. Poetry, then, is the only possible heaven. It must necessarily be the poetry of ourselves; its source is our imagination" (*LWS*, 360). At this time, Stevens was considering poetry as a substitute for religion, not as a variant of it. There is an element of escapism in the notion that the world is unendurable but for the poet's interpretation; poetry might then be another Marxian "opium of the people." In his essays, Stevens later tried to justify this escapism.

After 1928 the volume of his output increased, although slowly. Ultimately, the long rest period was followed by an eruption of poetry, resulting in three complete collections and one revised collection within three years. Both the sensuous imagery and the sense of forced innovation were gone. Stevens was dealing effectively with the challenge to his poetic that was coming from without and within. *Ideas of Order* is less concrete and more meditative than his earlier work and seems to have a new object of nostalgia—the loss of nature as a source of the divine, perhaps even the loss of the very paganism he so enthusiastically defines in "Sunday Morning." The emphasis shifts from the body, in the mind-body duality, to the mind. *Owl's Clover* (1936), partly a response to critics who accused Stevens of being an aesthete, verges on social commentary to the extent that Stevens later rejected from his *Collected Poems* (1954) what he called his "owlish" poems. *The Man with the Blue Guitar* (1937) is more intellectually complex and abstract than the earlier collections, but less overtly political than *Owl's Clover*. Throughout these three books, the element of the mystical or the transcendent diminishes, until in "Blue Guitar" Stevens arrives at the unequivocal substitute of the human imagination for the divine that he describes in the letter quoted above explaining this poem. The act of poetry becomes more and more a decreation. The apex of his involvement with the ordinary may be seen as the nadir of his transcendent vision.

By the time of *Ideas of Order*, Stevens had increased the proportion of explanation to demonstration in his work, making his poems more reflective and analytical. In few poems henceforth would a series of images carry the theme, as they do in "Hibiscus on the Sleeping Shores," "The Load of Sugar-Cane," and other *Harmonium* poems. He had moved away from what he considered the overlush and feminine nature of Florida to the North and the world of "men in crowds" (*CP*, 118). These collections show a rigorous defense of an activist poetic and an attempt to invest it with spiritual values. Nietzsche, Alfred North Whitehead, and William James seem to be the figures underlying this identification of poetry with force.[4] His earlier work seems to have equated the force of art with stylistic experiment. Now he focuses on the nature of the force itself, defining the art-force as a life-force, a "blessed rage."

The three books of poetry are all notes toward a definition of the imagination in its various engagements with the harsh realities of the time. The poems address certain questions: What is the imaginative life in a time when nothing is certain but change? What could be the justification for creating poetry in such times? If the romantic lark has been replaced by the humdrum jay, what kind of song will be produced? Poetry in an age without ideals becomes an attempt to distill the quintessentially human from the indiscriminate contemporary scene. This phase can be considered Stevens's humanist stage, the passage between the interrogation of the religious in *Harmonium* and its transformed reinstatement in *The Auroras of Autumn* (1950).

If the Florida poems of *Harmonium* provided one definition of poetry, these collections provide another and through it give poetry a practical function as well as an aesthetic one. Their goal is the justification of poetry in a time of trouble; to accomplish this goal, they must cast aside the ornamental and the elaborate. "The Man with the Blue Guitar" is Stevens's most unadorned work. It represents the bottom rung of his metaphysic, the point at which all earlier containers of transcendence have been emptied. What will come next must be the New Romantic of Joseph Carroll's exploration. The letters written during this period speak of the New Romantic as of a new dispensation, a replenishment of the romantic impulse that had been dispelled by the modern world. But in the letters as in the poems, concern with defining the New Romantic diminished as the poet's mind was forced by circumstances to engage more with the topical and the political.

Ideas of Order allows only a few glimpses of the envisioned New Romantic. For the most part, these are mind-poems meditating on the blank. There are no more bright flowers and birds, no more "concupiscent curds"; the high spirits and capers are gone. These poems have the pattern Stevens set early of making a tentative affirmation and then undercutting it, but the affirmations in this group are rare. Although "The Idea of Order at Key West" and a few other poems exalt the imagination's power, most of the poems regret its manifold failures and false starts. "Anglais Mort à Florence" speaks of the diminished or dwindled world of a man who "stood at last by God's help and the police," that is, by means of the established structures, but who "remembered a time when he stood alone" without crutches of any sort (*CP*, 149). "Sad Strains of a Gay Waltz" is similar in its reminiscent sadness; it mentions Hoon, the solipsistic reigning imagination of *Harmonium*, who "found all form and order in solitude" but for whom, now, "his forms have vanished" (*CP*, 121). Generally, the negative poems regret the loss of the moon hero, the romantic, who has no place in the contemporary aesthetic. Some of the poems express desire for the sun's incarnations to replace the moon's, that is, for a new manifestation of reality to be hailed and celebrated, as in "Ghosts as Cocoons." In general, *Ideas of Order* expresses a keen sense of disappointment, and whether this feeling of loss has to do with a marital or an aesthetic letdown is almost irrelevant.[5] Desire remains strong, although its obscure object is eclipsed.

The woman as muse and other appears far less frequently in *Ideas of Order*, in keeping with Stevens's desire to depart from the geography of Florida, but she is still there beneath his new concerns. She surfaces as the desired bride of "Ghosts as Cocoons" and as the singer of the sea in "The Idea of Order at Key West." Still, these are what Stevens might have thought of as "masculine" poems, poems of mind and will in which feeling and intuition are secondary. And even more than in *Harmonium*, the tone is often elegiac. These poems proclaim that something vital has been lost and a search is on for a replacement, but that the chance of finding a satisfactory one is slim. The romantic is what has been lost, and only the romantic, reenvisioned and renewed, can take its place. This romantic is harder to find than the slovenly muse of Florida, and harder to define than paganism.

"Farewell to Florida," the opening poem, directly states the intended new direction of Stevens's exploration. The South, the feminine sensuous, is to be left behind; its voice is to be sloughed off like a snake's skin and the speaker is to go north for his new subject and base. The South now seems to be an Eden of death, a lotus-eater land where passivity results in paralysis. (The snake's sloughing off of his skin is a recurrent symbol of renewal in Stevens, but the snake becomes a more multifaceted and subtle image in his later work.) Florida's sensuous nature is too alien and too engulfing for this awakened speaker; his former love for her has turned to antipathy and revulsion. Henceforth, the speaker promises to be the voice of the North. His new subject will be the actions and reactions of men, and his poetry will be of masculine motives and movements. "My North is leafless and lies in a wintry slime / Both of men and clouds, a slime of men in crowds." This new world, the North of cold and leaflessness, will free him to "return to the violent mind / That is their mind" (*CP*, 118). The speaker addresses the "high ship" that carries him to his new destination. This image too, that of a man with a craft he is sailing into new and unknown waters, recurs throughout Stevens's work, echoing Tennyson's "Ulysses." It becomes a major metaphor of transformative perception in the late poem "Prologues to What Is Possible."

At this stage, Stevens's poems as well as his letters claim that the desire for the transcendent and the numinous cannot be evaded, but that these qualities must be reinvested in something without claptrap, without visible falsity. "Sailing after Lunch" both explains and demonstrates this perspective. Stevens described this work as a poem that "perhaps . . . means more to me than it should," and he was unusually explicit in explaining it as an expression of the necessity of "keeping the romantic pure: eliminating from it what people think of as the romantic" (*LWS*, 276–77). Why did Stevens believe that he liked the poem more than it deserved? Perhaps because he found it too direct, too revealing, even though what it revealed remained central to his thought.

"Sailing after Lunch" takes the queasiness evoked by the notion of a postprandial sailing expedition as the feeling of the poet in our time—an uneasy sailor on an old boat that "goes round on a crutch" and will not launch properly. Uncharacteristically personal, the poem declares that its speaker is "a most inappropriate man / In a most unpropitious place." The poet's "prayer" or fervent desire is for the romantic; it "ought to be everywhere" (*CP*, 120). But it must not stay, and it must not return; it cannot be a historical romantic but must present, as a total immersion in reality, a participation that cannot be mediated through human interpretation (Carroll, 67–68). Its goal is "to expunge all people and be a pupil / Of the gorgeous wheel" (*CP*, 121). This is the sun worship of "Sunday Morning" again, but here the activity is more clearly symbolic.

To be a pupil of the wheel is to be tutored by the sun-source itself, but perhaps there is a double meaning to "pupil," recalling the Emersonian "transparent eyeball" and the transcendentalist's natural religion, which may be compared with Stevens's own earlier versions of natural religion (Carroll, 90–91). As in "Sunday Morning," the reward for discarding the outworn and accepting change as the only permanence is freedom and an enhanced sense of reality. "Sailing after Lunch," however, wholly lacks the sense of elegy found in "Sunday Morning" (and in most of the other poems of *Ideas of Order*). The poem expresses not nostalgia but the strong resolve to turn away deliberately from nostalgia. The hard-won freedom it claims is joy, a sense of immanence and the potency of presence, the ability to "rush brightly through the summer air" (*CP*, 121). This concluding image seems to have a woman concealed in it and may suggest a Stevensian notion of the "feminine" or feeling-toned experience of immediate participation.

If poetry is to usurp the function of religion, then there must be a theodicy for it. Such can be found in "The Idea of Order at Key West," perhaps the most anthologized poem of this group. The participants in this poem play out the drama of the creative engagement of mind and world. "She," the speaker, the sea, and "Ramon Fernandez" demonstrate how the imagination enhances reality without falsifying it. The poem begins with the unbridgeable gulf between mind and world and attempts to define the dynamics of their interaction.

> She sang beyond the genius of the sea.
> The water never formed to mind or voice,
> Like a body wholly body, fluttering
> Its empty sleeves; and yet its mimic motion
> Made constant cry, caused constantly a cry,
> That was not ours, although we understood,
> Inhuman, of the veritable ocean. (*CP*, 128)

There is a "genius" or presiding spirit to nature, but its cry is "not ours"; it is nature's own impenetrable utterance. (Compare this evocation of nature's voice with that of one of Stevens's last poems, "This Region November," in which the mind at the end of its existence in time listens in near despair to this other language.) The woman identified only as "she" sings "beyond the genius of the sea" and in so doing changes nothing but what is in the mind; her song is like reality, but it is not the same as reality. The imagination is not the voice of reality, "the dark voice of the sea." Neither is it our own understandings of reality, "her voice and ours." Rather, it is the intensification of reality that is given from the imagination's engagement with it. The tragic sense of life's evanescence is heightened: "It was her voice that made / The sky acutest at its vanishing" (*CP*, 129). The speaker then addresses Ramon Fernandez, whose name Stevens claimed to have chosen more or less at random but who is actually a French critic with whose work Stevens was familiar (*LWS*, 798, 823). Fernandez's criticism, which Stevens read in *Nouvelle revue française* as well as in English translation, does involve theories of perception as well as commentary on the relationship between poetry and social reality (Longenbach, 161). Perhaps, however, Fernandez, in a broad sense, is "the critic" or the theorist of poetry. He is asked for an explanation of how it could come about that those who heard the song found nature reordered or rearranged:

> . . . tell why the glassy lights,
> The lights in the fishing boats at anchor there,
> As the night descended, tilting in the air,
> Mastered the night and portioned out the sea,
> Fixing emblazoned zones and fiery poles,
> Arranging, deepening, enchanting night. (*CP*, 130)

It is the perceiver and not the critic, however, who provides the answer. The critic is instructed by the perceiver, who attributes the reordering of nature to desire so intense that it is designated a "blessed rage":

> Oh! Blessed rage for order, pale Ramon,
> The maker's rage to order words of the sea,
> Words of the fragrant portals, dimly-starred,
> And of ourselves and of our origins,
> In ghostlier demarcations, keener sounds. (*CP*, 130)

The revision is all in the perception; the "lights" cause it. The poem uses images of geometry to show the radical change in the perceived world as a result of the woman's song. It is this "blessed rage for order," the fierce vision of the "maker," that is responsible for a life lived in full awareness. The "rage for order" causes the creation of that intense poetry ("keener sounds") of our scarcely understood origins and points of departure. These portals are vague, barely discernible ("dimly-starred"), but marked out. The blessed rage drives toward their articulation, their definition ("ghostlier demarcations"). "Ghostlier" suggests both shadowy and spiritual, as in the German *geistlich*. This poem includes one of

Stevens's earlier suggestions that the poetic impulse is a hallowed one, sanctioned. The results of this "blessed rage" are a redefinition, or perhaps a more precise understanding, of what it is to be human. "The Idea of Order at Key West" is an early articulation of the ideas that invention is discovery and insights are genuine revelations. The demarcations are there; they are the to-be-discovered to which the "blessed rage" leads.

"The Idea of Order at Key West" reaches a pitch of exaltation not found in many other Stevens poems of the era. Significantly, he said very little about the poem afterward, and then almost always only in answer to direct questions about it. The intensity of its desire is rare in *Ideas of Order*, and it is not followed by a hasty retreat from its assertion, as is often the case in other poems. Stevens's usual concern was the challenge to the imagination posed by the bankruptcy of contemporary life, a problem he was to develop in its full complexity in "The Man with the Blue Guitar." (His reaction to the problem changes from the bitter disgust of the interim poems to the fullest engagement with the ordinary. In "An Ordinary Evening in New Haven," for example, the surface level of daily life becomes suffused with the imaginative source that feeds it.)

In *Harmonium*, the vulgar is the main obstacle to the imaginative life. In the poems of the three following collections, there are the additional obstacles of both kinds of depression. The poems repeatedly express the recognition that art, or at least the traditional approach to art, does not suffice. Nor are verbal highjinks and sensuous pleasures the remedy for the twentieth century's malaise. The only way to deal with the negative realities of the present is to accept them as the base of reality with which the imagination must deal. The impoverished present lacks a vitalizing myth; it is up to the poet to produce such a myth, and he cannot do it by falsifying the base of reality that it must reflect and enhance; to do so would be to create the sort of bogus pleasure-dome imagined by *Harmonium*'s "Ordinary Women." The vastness and complexity of the project sometimes produce exaltation and sometimes the dejection of defeat. When the project seems an impossibility, the poems are elegiac, looking back at a time when poetry at least appeared to be possible. In the more positive ones, they become invocations to the contemporary muse.

Some of the poems are overlaid by an irony that is one of the many means by which Stevens habitually distances himself from his subject and perhaps equally from himself. "Botanist on Alp (No. 1)," for instance, begins with the flat announcement that "Panoramas are not what they used to be" and notes, combining tongue in cheek with serious reflection, that "Marx has ruined Nature, / For the moment" (*CP*, 134). European civilization is dead, "The hotel is boarded and bare." But

> . . . the panorama of despair
> Cannot be the specialty
> Of this ecstatic air. (*CP*, 134)

However exhausted the tradition is, the force that drives it is renewable and renewing; reformation or re-formation is always possible. Marx's ban on intellectual indulgence is only temporary, and something will supplant it. Yet the vague affirmation at the end of this poem is unusual for *Ideas of Order* and may not be persuasive.

Perhaps the most elaborate exploration of the attempt to find a new way to participate in the present is the longest poem of the collection, "Like Decorations in a Nigger Cemetery." The title itself suggests Stevens's preoccupation with the idea that the imagination produces ornaments that stand out against the background of death, the ultimate poverty—"Ach, Mutter, this old black dress / I've been embroidering French flowers on it." (The above may be Stevens's version of Bergson's definition of the motive for human action: "Our action thus proceeds from 'nothing' to 'something' and its very essence is to embroider 'something' on the canvas of 'nothing'" [Fisher, 165]).

Such a function for art is limited, dismissable, if the product does not come from a master imagination, like the sheets on which the dead woman had "embroidered fantails once" in "The Emperor of Ice-Cream." The title "Like Decorations" is an example of Stevens's characteristic ironic distancing, the humility of a speaker who represents himself as Peter Quince in "Peter Quince at the Clavier" and deliberately calls the validity of the whole project into question. The title asks, Are not these fragments merely colorful figures to disguise the void, decorations in a cemetery? In a letter, Stevens describes the cemetery decorations as "litter"; in another, he describes his dislike of the word (and presumably the concept of) "decorative" (*LWS*, 272, 288). And yet, the cemetery decorations are necessary, products of hope and desire like the embroidered sheets and the "French flowers" sewn on the "old black dress" of "Explanation." Stevens may have felt that his work had been relegated to the status of decorations when he claimed that a critic thought he "had produced a lot of Easter eggs" (*LWS*, 314). Stevens's use of the pejorative label in the title of "Like Decorations in a Nigger Cemetery" shrieks at today's reader and undermines the poem. In fact, the use of this word must have raised eyebrows even in 1935, particularly as part of a literary poem. It may have been in part an attempt to shock, a left-over impulse from the era of Dadaism. Stevens's own attitudes about racial issues were equivocal and have been much debated. His stereo-types are part of his tendency to merge people and their landscapes, to claim "the gods come out of the weather." Africa is to him a place where natives are not to be divided from nature. Stevens's poems show a vitali-ty in the African imagination not shared by played-out Europe and equally unavailable to the speaker. Therefore, he remains an outsider to it, somewhat envious of the *participation mystique* that remains closed to him because of what he thinks of as his alienating sophistication. Here he represents the "decorations" as products of an imagination not his own, or not predominantly his own, distancing his proposals and allow-ing himself to offer them offhandedly, without commitment.

This poem begins with the image of Whitman evoked as a kind of muse, bearing the energy of creation/procreation.

> In the far South the sun of autumn is passing
> Like Walt Whitman walking along a ruddy shore. . . .
> Nothing is final, he chants. No man shall see the end.
> His beard is of fire and his staff is a leaping flame. (*CP*, 150)

Stevens's Whitman suggests a wholeness to the natural system. Whitman's world is an organism whose self-renewal provides a mathe-matics that factors in the negative of death without reducing the prod-uct to zero. Thus, the poem has affinities with the earlier "Sunday Morning," but instead of a structured argument, it contains short, evocative segments that explore the ways of reacting to death. They are a scattering of examples, minisermons, epigrams, reflections. Some of the sections allude to the actual cemetery (for example, in part 14, "The leaden pigeon on the entrance gate"), but most do not. In discussing this collection, Stevens commented, "I ought to say that it is a habit with me to be thinking of some substitute for religion" (*LWS*, 348). That state-ment defines his position at this point—he is not seeking a new religion, like paganism, but a substitute for it. This replacement must satisfy the needs that Christianity satisfied, without sharing what Stevens thought to be the flaws of Christianity.

"Like Decorations" suggests a series of these substitutes, none of which is fully satisfactory. There is philosophy (part 9); full participation in the present (parts 28, 26, and so on); art (part 38); anthropomorphic gods (part 42); music (part 48); poetry (part 32). Poetry seems to receive the most favor as consolation, although its life too is transient. It is an intense moment of involvement:

> Poetry is a finikin thing of air
> That lives uncertainly and not for long
> Yet radiantly beyond much lustier blurs. (*CP*, 155)

The thesis underlying the poem, however, is most completely expressed in its last section:

> Union of the weakest develops strength
> Not wisdom. Can all men, together, avenge
> One of the leaves that have fallen in autumn?
> But the wise man avenges by building his city in snow. (*CP*, 158)

Perhaps the "union of the weakest" alludes to leftist coalitions, as suggested by the critic Stanley Burnshaw (whose comments on Stevens's *Ideas of Order* spurred the poet to write *Owl's Clover*).[6] It is likely to be a more general allusion, however, suggesting that social action is not relevant to art or philosophy, or merely that it takes a single mind to achieve vision. The poem argues that strength is no defense against death. The only "wisdom" is to build the city in snow: to accept transience as the necessary base and material of all created structure. To do this opens new vistas for the arts, whose foundations were formerly various rigid structures that could not endure the various shiftings of the landscape. "Unions" of whatever sort can do nothing against death; the wise man, by accepting death as the basis and underpinning of life, lives more fully because he lives realistically. Thus, if the poem offers no "substitute" for religion, it outlines the parameters of such a substitute and suggests what it has to do.

Ideas of Order does not fulfill the second part of the promise it makes in its opening poem. It does leave Florida behind, and its speakers no longer steep themselves in the swamp and describe the lures and repulsions of the lush southern muse. But the collection does not yet engage in its promised

> . . . return to the violent mind
> That is their mind, these men, and that will bind
> me round. (*CP*, 117)

Rather, these are still valedictory poems, commemorating the losses of all the certainties. Frost, one of Stevens's persistent death elements, recurs often. Meanings slip away from their moorings, so that not even language is reliable, although it has more permanence than other things. Typical in tone and attitude of much of this work are "A Postcard from the Volcano" and "Autumn Refrain." "Postcard" begins

> Children picking up our bones
> Will never know that these were once
> As quick as foxes on the hill. . . . (*CP*, 158)

The speaker, using a "we" that is neither royal nor editorial but referring to a generation, explores the paradox that when the present becomes the past, its imprint is left but not the spirit of the imprinter, so that language grows by accretion:

> Children,
> Still weaving budded aureoles,
> Will speak our speech and never know. . . . (*CP*, 159)

The poem combines elegy and paean as it mourns and celebrates language, time's human witness. Today's speakers will leave, will be bones for children to pick up, but nevertheless, these children will look at the "mansion" and say it seems as if it is still somehow inhabited. They

> Will say of the mansion that it seems
> As if he that lived there left behind
> A spirit storming in blank walls. . . . (*CP*, 159)

as if the words of things did in fact contain the spirit of their speaker. "A Postcard from the Volcano" is also a poem of the hallowing of language, the impulse to speech. The "aureoles" and the bones picked up by children, suggestive of the relics of saints, imply a beatification. Not only the rage for order is "blessed" but the means of achieving it. Still, the tone of the poem is elegiac; there is a strong note of *ave atque vale* to it. If poetry is being offered as a replacement for religion, what is really being honored is human articulation of loss.

The conflict and paradox of the poet's project appears in "Autumn Refrain," an autumnal poem written before the summer of Stevens's career. The speaker looks at the waste of the demythologized world and

seeks the source that informs all myths. It is evening, and the works of
the sun have gone, as have the day birds, the grackles. The night bird,
the nightingale, is inappropriate for the speaker. The nightingale, bird
of romance, can sing only "evasions." So far there is nothing new here
for Stevens. The romantic, he pronounces elsewhere, is "purely the
vapidest fake."

Yet beneath the silence of the debunked, deromanticized scene is
noise, or music, or undeciphered message:

> And yet beneath
> The stillness of everything gone, and being still,
> Being and sitting still, something resides,
> Some skreaking and skrittering residuum. . . . (*CP*, 160)

The "residuum"—chemically, the irreducible minimum, the "quantity or
body of matter remaining after evaporation, combustion, distillation, or
the like"[7]—turns out to have a voice. It is this voice that speaks, that
"grates the evasions of the nightingale," and belies romance: "And the
stillness is in the key, all of it is, / The stillness is all in the key of that
desolate sound" (*CP*, 160). The silence of the bare world counteracts
imagination's projections, but it contains its own tone that is an alien
voice and timbre. Thus, it is desolate; it excludes the speaker. And yet it
is the key—musical tone and final resolution—of the world's language
and silence.

In *Ideas of Order*, *Harmonium*'s gaudiness has given way to a serious
engagement with what Stevens will ultimately call the "plain sense of
things" (*CP*, 502). He no longer complains of the banal and the boring
as blocks to creativity. He accepts these as the poet's essential building
materials. These poems look at the nature of the imaginative processes
that make life endurable. In his next two collections, Stevens approaches
a definition of the imaginative that is grounded in and limited to the
material world.

Chapter Three

"Things as They Are":
Owl's Clover and
The Man with the Blue Guitar

Stevens settled into his carefully edited life in which business and family concerns were sufficiently in order to allow him time and space to write. Recalling these years at the Hartford, his coworkers commented on how demanding he was about his own work and about theirs, and how little they knew of his doings as a poet. He had his secretary at the office transcribe his poetry, but he did not discuss it. Sometimes, however, he would show his colleagues some of the art that his newly acquired financial ease allowed him to acquire.[1] Much of his satisfaction seems to have come from the material world at this time; he meant it when he wrote, "Money is a kind of poetry" (*OP*, 191).

Regularity was the hallmark of Stevens's daily life. Scheduling and a certain inflexibility allowed him his success; only later would he find that "a violent order is disorder" (*CP*, 215). If his personal life was a great disappointment to him, he generally kept any such feelings to himself. But the beautiful muse disappeared from his work at least temporarily, and he looked instead to the male myth as source for poetry. The new poetry, however, lacks the emotional heights and depths of his earlier work. "The Man with the Blue Guitar" does not take any risks. Clearly, Stevens was attempting to deal with the real world in his poetry also.

In *Owl's Clover* (1936) and *The Man with the Blue Guitar* (1937), Stevens fully engages the question of finding an appropriate voice for the twentieth century. He now defines specifically what kinds of sounds will best testify for and represent his time. *Owl's Clover* is more argumentative and deals directly with the issues raised by critics during the Great Depression, when some held that poetry is self-indulgent or at best irrelevant unless its goal is social action. In the poems of *Owl's Clover*, Stevens claims that the prevalence of human misery might change the perception of poetry but does not obviate its value. *The Man with the Blue Guitar* also raises issues of daily economic matters, but it is more metaphorical than direct, and it focuses more on the flexibility of language, exploring what sounds are appropriate for a demythologized and ordinary world. "The Man with the Blue Guitar" strips layers of interpretation from the hypothetical, central real. Standing at the very bottom of Stevens's ladder of transcendence, "Blue Guitar" represents some of his most negative comments on traditional religion and expresses doubt over the possibility of achieving any kind of transcendent vision. This dismissal of the spiritual is also found in his letters, particularly those that discuss the meaning of "Blue Guitar."

Ideas of Order began the attempt to incorporate the topical with the aesthetic, but when this collection was criticized for its apparent aestheticism, Stevens made even more explicit attempts to justify poetry, and his own poetry in particular, against attackers. Poetry has a valuable function, he asserted, even in times of depression or war. It may be that Stanley Burnshaw and other critics who found *Ideas of Order* evasive did Stevens a favor in forcing him to rework his aesthetic, tightening and justifying his position in the face of their opposition. Although Stevens had long abandoned the idea of an Eden of the senses (to the extent that he had ever entertained such a picture), his critics believed he had not gone far enough toward "the world of men in crowds," for he did not take up membership in the crowd. Thus, he found it increasingly necessary to defend and explain his distance to a hostile and suspicious left. He conducted his defense in both poetry and prose, and doing so brought him fully into the world of "things as they are." Critics such as James Longenbach and Alan Filreis, who focus on Stevens's interactions with the forces and events of his time, explain insightfully this period of his work, but it would be a mistake to find it a stopping place.[2] His critics challenged him by accusing him of a tendency to aestheticize pain and to look toward a "pure poetry" as solace, instead of advocating poetry that calls for constructive action. His measured response was an attempt to convince them, and perhaps himself, that he was not guilty of a negative escapism. But the decreated world he offered as poetic subject and object could not take the place of the imagined one.

As the reviews of *Ideas of Order* demonstrated, Stevens was now being taken seriously by the literary world, and henceforth he was treated not as an interesting newcomer but as a major poet. Nevertheless, praise by figures like Marianne Moore and Howard Baker was offset by criticism from the left, resulting in Stevens's poetic engagement with the apostles of Marxism and those poets attracted by the literary leftism of the 1930s. Theodore Roethke, for instance, said of *Ideas of Order*, "It is a pity that such a rich and special sensibility should be content with the order of words and music, and not project itself more vigorously upon the present-day world."[3] In particular, Stanley Burnshaw's 1935 review in *New Masses* caused the poet to examine and explain his positions. According to Burnshaw, Stevens was not confronting the realities of the time but attempting confusedly to reconcile an idea of purist art with a society to which such art was clearly no longer appropriate. "Realists have been bitter at the inanity of Pope's 'Whatever is, is right,'" he wrote, "but Stevens plunges ahead to the final insolence: 'For realists, what is is what should be'" (62). Although he was speaking of *Ideas of Order*, he could have been aptly describing the spirit of "The Emperor of Ice-Cream." The nation's hungry could not be expected to bow down to this emperor.

This dismissive response came at a time when the literary left was at a high point of influence and importance, and the implication that he was not a genuine realist must have stung Stevens. It was not possible for Stevens to overlook the accusation that he was evading the universal responsibility of the serious artist to work for social justice, at least if he wished to be a poetic spokesman for anyone besides an elitist literary establishment. He thus engaged the critics directly in the series of poems published as *Owl's Clover* in 1936. In these, he attempts to discuss the relationship between art and society, showing the delicate and shifting relationship between the creator of the work of art and the place into which the work must fit. Later he revised the poems to eliminate the figure of Mr. Burnshaw and to soften other explicit topical references, and he dropped the poems entirely when selecting for his *Collected Poems*. The poems received little critical attention until a focus on the pressure of history on literature foregrounded them in the late 1980s.[4] In fact, they have little power as poetry, although they do elucidate Stevens's politics. Compared with *The Man with the Blue Guitar*, they may illustrate Yeats's dictum that "we make out of the quarrel with others, rhetoric; but out of the quarrel with ourselves, poetry."

"The Irrational Element in Poetry," an essay with which Stevens introduced a reading of some of the poems from *Owl's Clover*, throws some light on the poems. Freud, Rimbaud, and Mallarmé had been major influences favoring the irrational in poetry, Stevens noted. He explained that the issue addressed in "The Old Woman and the Statue" is the effect of the depression on the interest in art (*OP*, 226). Traditional art is no longer relevant to the observer because of the tension of the present, the essay claimed. The present requires new, renewing approaches;

indeed, "one of the motives in writing is renewal" (*OP*, 226), and this renewal is of the art as well as of the artist. Stevens then discussed an essay he had recently read that claimed that one writes poetry to find God, concluding himself that one writes to find that good "which, in the Platonic sense, is synonymous with God." He was still concerned with finding a substitute for God, but he seemed in this comment to be blurring the distinction between finding the substitute and finding God. Thus, the poet's function and indeed his duty is to resist the pressure of "ominous and destructive circumstance"; he is to find order in disorder. It goes without saying that fulfilling this obligation does not involve forcing an arbitrary order on disorder, but rather being constantly in tune with reality to represent appropriately the natural orders within it. Even the poet's language and the general function of language are determined by the nature of the time period. "There is, in short, an unwritten rhetoric that is always changing and to which the poet must always be turning" (*OP*, 231). Stevens's 1930s and 1940s poetics contain what came to be elements of New Historicist literary theory.

The irrational, then, becomes a way of approaching the disorder of experience so as to find meaning in it. Art is not an evasion of reality, or a falsification of it, but an exhaustive (and exhausting) search through it for whatever truth it may contain. This search is both a natural impulse and a moral imperative. It is, in fact, how the artist serves society. Stevens initially wanted to call the *Owl's Clover* collection *Aphorisms on Society*, which shows how far he was willing to sacrifice poetry to argument. In accepting his second-choice name, he commented, "The point of this group in any case is to try to make poetry out of commonplaces: the day's news; and that surely is owl's clover" (*LWS*, 311). "Owl's clover" is false clover. The day's news, the ordinary, constitutes the false clover from which the true must be gleaned. The poems argue that the artist does, in fact, include the sadness of the world in his art, but not necessarily in the obvious ways preferred by leftists. Moreover, the poems suggest that the leftists have a tunnel vision that prevents them from seeing the value of the nonpragmatic, nonutilitarian approach to art. Burnshaw interrogates the statue; in finding its flaws, he misses the value of the impulse that created it and continues to create and renew the world for the sensitive observer.

Stevens's comment on the first of the five poems in *Owl's Clover* is relevant not only for how it explains the poem but for what it indicates about his concepts of the function of art at the time. "Although this ["The Old Woman and the Statue"] deals specifically with the status of art in a period of depression, it is, when generalized, one more confrontation of reality (the depression) and the imagination (art). A larger expression than confrontation is: a phase of the universal intercourse. There is a flow to and fro between reality and the imagination" (*LWS*, 368).

This "universal intercourse" is apparent in the poem by the shifts from the old woman, "the bitter mind / In a flapping cloak" (*OP*, 76), whose entire focus is on her need, to the marble statue of the horses, and back to the woman. The sculptor had blended his creation into the surroundings so that it belongs to the landscape. He had not foreseen the "bitter mind" of the woman that changes the horses from their "moving colors" to the "black of what she thought." The statue, though, does have an effect on her, changed as it is by her perception: "It was as if transparence touched her mind" (*OP*, 77). The last section of the poem provides a hypothetical scene from which the woman has vanished. The horses would then revert to their original impression of strength and nobility. Stevens commented, in discussing the poem, "There is conflict between the rise of a lower class, with all its realities, and the indulgences of an upper class. . . . While there is a conflict, it is not an essential conflict. The conflict is temporary. The only possible order of life is one in which all order is incessantly changing" (*LWS*, 291–92). His attitude that "this too will pass" would not have satisfied Burnshaw.

Of "Mr. Burnshaw and the Statue," Stevens explained that, since Burnshaw had applied the perspective of communism to his poetry, he intended to "apply the point of view of a poet to Communism" (*LWS*, 289). The poem begins with an observer (Burnshaw?) examining the statue and finding it useless, futile.

> The thing is dead. . . . Everything is dead
> Except the future. Always everything
> That is is dead except what ought to be.
> All things destroy themselves or are destroyed. (*OP*, 78)

The statue is dead art; it has no interest to the present. There appears to be a change in the meditator's perspective after the first four lines, from that of a possible Burnshaw to that of a more general critic, one who provides an argumentative counterpoint, as does the voice responding to the woman in "Sunday Morning." This answering voice comments on this art's impermanence. The horses are falsifications made by a craftsman who was merely following a recipe and who never knew inspiration.

> They might be sugar or paste or citron-skin
> Made by a cook that never rode the back
> Of his angel through the skies. (*OP*, 78)

The resulting statue is a mere toy, "a thing from Schwarz's." The horses should reflect the reality of their time, but instead they are only "the jottings-down of the sculptor's foppishness" (*OP*, 78), and they have nothing to outlast the living horses on which the artwork is based. The future will find it gone, as it should be.

The second section calls for divine "sibilant requiems for this effigy" that no romance can reawaken to life. Reality will always outlast its myths—the "Sunday Morning" theme again.

> Agree: the apple in its orchard, round
> And red, will not be rounder, redder then
> Than now. (*OP*, 79)

The statue is to be replaced by something that does reflect the time.

> The stones
> That will replace it shall be carved, "The Mass
> Appoints These Marbles Of Itself To Be
> Itself." (*OP*, 80)

In this popularized form of art, it is the mass, not a single heroic figure, that is commemorated in stone. The art is nothing more or less than its era. In an era blind to art, to which art is irrelevant, products substitute for art. The poetic of such an era might call for not a supreme but a workaday fiction, with the demands that "it must be concrete, it must provide discomfort, and it must be set in stone."

The next section discusses the relationship between poetry and politics, ideas of order and the chaos to which they are applied. The irony is that poets' politics, if applied, would create a world impossible for poets, since poets are not of the world and any order is a falsification of their vision. Disorder is a form of order—an idea Stevens develops in later poems. The goal, then, is discovery rather than imposition. The next section, part 5, factors death into this order/disorder system. The "trash can at the end of the world" contains everything, rich and poor, sculptor and art. Here where all is reduced to nothing the plans for material progress are seen as worth no more than anything else. The concluding sections arrive at a position like that of the sun-dance in "Sunday Morning," except that here what is being discarded is not so much religion as social programming. There is an individual truth, a "true meridian / that is yourselves" (*OP*, 83), and that comes from acceptance of the unalterability of the human situation. "It is only enough / To live incessantly in change" (*OP*, 82). The maidens' dance of this passage is participation in this flux. (Although it is subdued almost to dullness in contrast to the "boisterous devotions to the sun" of the male worshipers in "Sunday Morning.")

"The Greenest Continent" compares religions and their places; the African god of primitive reality is contrasted with the empty heaven of Europe, for which traditional religion no longer has life. The vulgar contemporary and the shocks of war showed up the false premises and promises of European Christianity. Its vitality was sapped by multiple causes: "Everything did it at last" (*OP*, 84). Ironically, the metaphor is economic; the old world and its ways cost too much: "The heaven of Europe is empty, like a Schloss / Abandoned because of taxes" (*OP*, 84). But "there was a heaven once," a momentarily satisfying relation between mind and world, perceiver and perceived. This "heaven" was neither European nor African, Africa being a place where the most primitive impulses are reflected in its chthonic, vital, yet death-dealing gods; it was a true relation between the individual self and the mystery of the other. The poem posits a war between the African imagination and the European celestial inhabitants: "Hé quoi! Angels go pricking elephants? / Wings spread and whirling over jaguar-men?" (*OP*, 87). The ridiculousness of such a conflict shows up the European angelic aggressors as belonging to "concentric bosh," the whole discarded system of the geocentric universe. The statue fares little better than European Christianity if the statue is transplanted to Africa: if the gods do not partake of their place, if they do not come from their weather, then they are not "the spirit's natural images." The marble horses do not fit the African imagination. Part 7 invokes another failure—the café intellectuals who have no gods but only talk, talk, talk. The poem concludes that the common god is "Fatal Ananke"—the African god of necessity, who contains all gods and is the determinant of all statues. Causality, the principle of natural law, is the one true "unmerciful pontifex" to whom all must submit. Africa is closer to the imagination's source than Europe, but its imagery is relentless (*OP*, 90).

Even more directly topical is "A Duck for Dinner," which reflects the Great Depression's political promise, "A chicken in every pot." The Bulgar is the voice of the proletariat, whose threatening voice Stevens heard in the *New Masses* review. This poem is a confrontation between Bulgar and Statue, the statue here representing not only art but the artist and the artistic process as well (*LWS*, 372).

The Bulgar sees the rise of the proletariat as a slow evolution toward full control, a gradual takeover of culture by the masses. "They rise a bit / On summer Sundays in the park" (*OP*, 91). These people are growing into their own, but their pleasures and pursuits are mass-produced. The Bulgar is contrasted in the second section with a more native American myth, the "buckskin . . . crosser of snowy divides" (*OP*, 91), the Paul Bunyan–type individualist who creates a new world from the blueprints of the old. The new masses cannot even begin to understand such a man:

> For you,
> Day came upon the spirit as life comes
> And deep winds flooded you; for these, day comes,
> A penny sun in a tinsel sky, unrhymed. (*OP*, 91)

In mythic figures such as these, there is no capacity for poetry. The lowering of imaginative sights is evident in the impact of the people on their place: "Apocalypse was not contrived for parks, / Geranium budgets, pay-roll water-falls" (*OP*, 93).

The next section explicitly reflects socialism, "the newest Soviet réclame," as a "profound abortion." The visionary has glimpsed the future, and it does not work: "Suppose the future fails" (*OP*, 93). The figure is then evoked of the appropriate carpetbagger hero for such people, a rhetorician, "some pebble-chewer practiced in Tyrian speech." The hot-air artist

> . . . spins a sphere
> Created, like a bubble, of bright sheens,
> With a tendency to bulge as it floats away. (*OP*, 94)

For such listeners, this treatment might be efficacious.

But the statue, in this poem not merely the artifact but both art and art's source, is foregrounded again in the next section, continuing to vitalize this new generation. It is a permanence:

> The statue is the sculptor not the stone.
> In this he carved himself, he carved his age,
> He carved the feathery walkers standing by . . .
> Exceeding sex, he touched another race. (*OP*, 95)

Going beyond sex, as Stevens himself explained, to have "progeny by the spirit" (*LWS*, 372), the authentic artist creates that which can touch future generations. Art is there in this real sense for everyone; as an enrichment it provides "For the million, perhaps, two ducks instead of one, / More of ourselves" (*OP*, 95). Such a creator is a kind of savior. The poem concludes with a scene that is a combination of elegy for the past and yearning for the future. If the present is inhospitable to art, when, and how, shall we fulfill our need for it?

> Where shall we find more than derisive words?
> When shall lush chorals spiral through our fire
> And daunt that old assassin, heart's desire? (*OP*, 96)

The source of that possible future satisfaction remains ambiguous, whether it comes from outside or wells from the heart. But the rhyme that ends the poem points to a climax of longing that the seeker be in some sense found, his voice answered by a richer voice.

"Sombre Figuration," the last poem, looks into the subconscious as a source of fulfillment. The "subman" is another figure for the imagination, this time a kind of race-memory that seems to correspond to the Jungian collective unconscious. The rationalist, "the man that thinks" (*OP*, 96), has grown wearisome—the reason falsifies. "The man below," however, "imagines and it is true" (*OP*, 96). This subman, the "anti-logician," thinks without rules; his associations are surrealistic assemblages of traces in the race-memory. He is "the Irrational" of the surrealists and of Stevens's essay. His images "surprise the sterile rationalist," who never knew there could be this kind of truth beneath the surface. The eruption of the subconscious removes the useless structures of past orders and reconciles conscious and unconscious. The remainder of the poem illustrates Stevens's comment on it: "The future must bear within it every past, not least the pasts that have become submerged in the sub-conscious, things in the memory of races. We fear because we remember" (*LWS*, 373). Seen from this perspective, through the eyes of the subman, the statue insists on its reality; it does not belong in the world of the subconscious. The poet has taken a part of Crispin's journey again and gone too far into moonland; the antidote is to return to the everyday, the place he calls "hum-drum space." From there, desire renews itself, the desire, which can never be fulfilled, to be and live in reality.

Stevens's engagement with the left clearly did not fully satisfy him; he returned to these themes repeatedly. *Owl's Clover*'s main appeal has been to historicist critics who see in it a more direct attempt than Stevens usually made to engage with the facts of his era. Its argument finally suggests that the leftist solutions are structures that, like Stevens's discarded Christianity, falsify by imposing artificial order.[5] These poems claim that true art involves discovery, not imposition. Their interest is in the position they play in Stevens's development: they show the bankruptcy of the materialistic imagination by example as well as in their argument—they remain rhetoric, after all. Moreover, their patterns are basically similar. They proceed from a relatively straightforward confrontation through various possible solutions, which are unfinished and/or unsatisfactory, to an ambiguous conclusion of rhapsodic intensity. Only the last one brings the argument back to earth, leaving us with "the medium man among other medium men" (OP, 101).

If reading the collection produces confusion rather than satisfaction, it may be because Stevens himself was ambivalent about the issues and uncertain of his own conclusions. Imagination is represented variously in the poems: a limited individual imagination, a kind of collective imagination, and imagination as an undefined force that nevertheless dwarfs the others and remains the most powerful drive and satisfaction. Stevens is not yet willing to define imagination as God, or as anything beyond the human, but he wishes to define it as fully human and yet without human limitations.

The questions addressed in *Owl's Clover* are also explored in the more widely known *The Man with the Blue Guitar*, but more subtly and more poetically. Here Stevens is honestly conducting the quarrel as much with himself as with the critics. "The Man with the Blue Guitar" is a series of 33 variations on a theme, but the music has changed drastically since the composition of "Peter Quince." This poem is harsh and discordant in its attempts to work out a role for the imagination vis-à-vis a distorted and disturbed present: the music has been adapted to the words. The 33 sections of couplets, varying in length and in their use of rhyme and meter, explore the ways the imagination may most fruitfully and truthfully engage reality. The title and the first section suggest, of course, the painting "The Old Guitarist" from Picasso's blue period. In fact, Stevens said, "I had no particular painting of Picasso's in mind" (*LWS*, 786), and he instructed the editors of an Italian translation of his poems not to print the painting with the poem. Nevertheless, the famous blue-tinged figure of the old man who appears nearly blind to reality as he produces his inner music is a dominant presence in the work. The ragged guitarist of the painting, sitting cross-legged in bleak surroundings, suggests through the angles of his posture an obliviousness to discomfort and poverty. Picasso and his art and aesthetic are alluded to elsewhere in the poem, but these references are mostly to Picasso's later stages, including (particularly) cubism. Stevens's comment may be taken to indicate that Picasso's art as a whole, not just the single picture called to mind by the title, was a generative force for the poem.

Stevens's guitarist, accused of not playing "things as they are," responds, "Things as they are / Are changed upon the blue guitar." The listeners, who are granted critic's rights, demand that he play

> A tune beyond us, yet ourselves,
> A tune upon the blue guitar
> Of things exactly as they are. (*CP*, 165)

Their desire seems to be impossible: they want a transformation, or a transcendence, that is yet the thing itself. The poem explores this possibility, using the chords and discords of the guitar to represent the various meetings between mind and world that the would-be music-maker tests and listens to in his search for the right sound.

The guitar player's first response to the demand for "a tune beyond us, yet ourselves," is a demurral: "I cannot bring a world quite round / Although I patch it as I can" (*CP*, 165). The notion of "patching" here enters Stevens's work, and it remains as a motif. Stevens's "patchwork" is an arrangement of parts to make something that is not quite a whole, and yet is more than the parts, perhaps a viable but not a supreme fiction. This idea appears later in "Parts of a World" and elsewhere. In part 2, he constructs a world that is not "quite round" and a man that is "a hero's head, large eye / And bearded bronze, but not a man," although his creator "reach[es] through him almost to man" (*CP*, 165). Creation in part 3 is destruction: just as the farmer nails the crow across the door to scare away other predators, so does the guitarist need to "lay the brain upon the board / And pick the acrid colors out" (*CP*, 166) if he is to play "man number one." Such violence results in a violent creation, discordant music. He then asks if "things as they are" are sufficient cause for poetry, and he looks at answers. In part 4, the speaker looks at the music of the many, the community: "A million people on one string" (*CP*, 166). This music is a "buzzing of the blue guitar"; it is not the harsh jangle that comes from the attempt to play "man number one" but something less intense, more common, like the flies that buzz "in autumn air" (*CP*, 166).

In part 5, he considers the poetry of the Christian tradition, "torches wisping in the underground . . . / structure of vaults upon a point of light" (*CP*, 167). The reality of Christianity, its spark, has been occasion for the huge "structure of vaults," suggesting the spheres within spheres of the Ptolemaic cosmos. For the speaker, this tradition is bankrupt; therefore, poetry that is humanized and humanistic must take the place of "empty heaven and its hymns." Now the guitar is "chattering" rather than buzzing or jangling; as the fiction approaches the human, the guitar approaches human speech. Stevens invariably brings the metaphysical into any discussion of the topical. The metaphysical surfaces frequently in *Owl's Clover*, even if it is presented as a ridiculous improbability or as a clash of myths—the angels giving chase to the reigning spirits of Africa, for instance. The metaphysical is never far from the surface in Stevens, and he cannot substitute social program for divine design. Useless, too, to argue that his celestial paraphernalia is only metaphor, for however fiercely he strips the nimbus from his angelic messengers, it slips back, if only in the exalted tone of his descriptions.

The next few segments of "Blue Guitar" explore the nature of the poetry that would suffice for our times and play with the contradictions involved in attempting poetry that is both "beyond us as we are / Yet nothing changed by the blue guitar." Poetry is, "for a moment, final." The oxymoron expresses the difficulty that in a world based on change, the highest values cannot rest on a notion of eternity. Through part 9, Stevens explores the notion of poetry as part of the real, a function of weather. But if the fiction is a function of weather, what of the poet? The impressionist Picasso painting reappears as stage, weather, and actor merge:

> The color like a thought that grows
> Out of a mood, the tragic robe
>
> Of the actor, half his gesture, half
> His speech, the dress of his meaning, silk
>
> Sodden with melancholy words,
> The weather of his stage, himself. (*CP*, 170)

This is the beginning of the evolution of the poet-hero figure who in various manifestations dominates the poetry of Stevens's next collections. He is a transformed Crispin at this point; Stevens now desires his figures to be fully human. They will become more abstract and exalted as the poems progress.

"Blue Guitar" then goes off in other directions to analyze elements of the creative process and to note some of the flaws that can creep into it. In part 10, the false hero or demagogue poet is attacked; his music is that of the "slick trombones" that have mass appeal but offer little to the discriminating. Part 11 describes apocalyptic change in such a way as to throw doubt on any attempt to chronicle it. The way time swallows up existence makes a dissonance of music. The guitarist keeps approaching and withdrawing from reality throughout the poem; part 12 is an attempt on the part of the artist to assert himself, although he cannot really determine what is self and what is art. The section explores the identity of self and voice, and the subtle differences between the two. Part 13 examines the excesses of uncontrolled romantic poetry. Among these come glimpses of the poet's true potential. Possibilities flash like fireworks and then fade, used up, taken beyond the intensity of their brightness. The sense of possibility alternates with the weight of futility. Part 14 expresses the value of the light of a single mind as perspective and illuminator. The candle and what it illumines appear frequently in Stevens, from the poems in the June Books of his courtship, through the flame of fragile individual consciousness in "Valley Candle," to the powerful candles of the last handful of poems in *The Collected Poems*, where the flickering light of the single mind blends into the flare of a greater intelligence, "the celestial possible." In part 14,

> A candle is enough to light the world.
> It makes it clear. Even at noon
> It glistens in essential dark. (*CP*, 172)

This candle remains a symbol of the individual imagination, as it is in "Valley Candle," but its power is enlarged. As it is all, it must be enough.

In part 15, the poet wonders, Will such a decadent and vulgar society not wear a poet down into an image of itself? He touches on this fear in the more public poems of *Owl's Clover*, but here he risks being personal, offering one of his rare uses of the first-person singular without a clearly identified distancing mask:

> Is this picture of Picasso's this "hoard
> Of destructions," a picture of ourselves,
>
> Now, an image of our society?
> Do I sit, deformed, a naked egg,
>
> Catching at Good-bye, harvest moon,
> Without seeing the harvest or the moon? (*CP*, 173)

The popular song (actually "Shine on, Harvest Moon") is an example of
the debasement of the reality of autumn, of cliché formation. Can the
poet retain his sensibilities when he cannot sever himself from a society
that seems to have none?

Further sections explore the relationships between the two parts of
the dualist universe, mind/body, imagination/reality, and the conflicts
between them. Part 16 looks at the way in which the particulars of the
negative reality block vision. Overly gritty reality calls for a hard-sur-
faced poetry. Other sections (17, 18) examine the relationship between
mind and body, spirit and substance, and chart the course of the imagination as it departs from the real. The series reaches a climax in part 19
as the poet articulates his goal:

> That I may reduce the monster to
> Myself, and then may be myself
>
> In face of the monster. . . .
>
> And play of the monster and of myself,
>
> Or better not of myself at all,
> But of that as its intelligence,
>
> Being the lion in the lute
> Before the lion locked in stone. (*CP*, 175)

Reality is the lion "locked in stone"; the imagination is "the lion in the
lute." This is the story of "The Idea of Order at Key West" retold as an
allegory of conquest, reduction, submission. Poetry has become a matter
of strength, not a matter of inspiration; it is more a confrontation than a
song, although it has music still. In commenting on this section, Stevens
said, "The mind of one man, if strong enough, can become master of all
the life in the world. . . . Any really great poet, musician, etc. does this"
(*LWS*, 360). The claim illustrates Stevens's aggressive humanism at this
point. Creative perception, he asserts, requires strength and persistence
as well as vision; it is active. He is advocating a muscular poetics.

From this extreme position the poem then withdraws. Parts 20 and
21 examine the self, the individual sentience as a replacement for the
gods, but they find the dwindled and ungraspable self resistant to myth.
Since the self as subject is undefinable, the poem returns to a definition
of poetry. Part 22 is particularly provocative: it talks about the "absence

in reality" that occurs between the issue and return of the poem from reality. This absence, this gap or hole, suggests the unbridgeable space between the real and the perceived world, the unknowable. The poem asks, Does the unknown otherness of reality inform the poem? There is no answer, nor can there be; but then the series proceeds to the other definition of the unknowable, death, and then back, in part 24, to embrace life as the source for poetry. The poet seizes and articulates life; the "hawk of life" is the thing seen, understood, and spoken with the joy of appropriation. There is a true confrontation between self and other, celebrated and ritualized in language (*CP*, 178).

The rhythm changes drastically as the poet becomes entertainer in the next turning. Stevens's tendency to step back from any precipice is evident throughout "Blue Guitar." Part 24 may be seen as the affirmative climax of the poem. After this section defines the poet (or poem) as a "hawk of life," the poet becomes a juggler, a comedian, in part 25; he imposes a comic order. But this description of poet-as-juggler is only an arpeggio; Stevens returns to a tone of modified exaltation in later segments. The world reasserts its primacy and opacity; yet in part 28 the poet claims: "I am a native in this world / And think in it as a native thinks" (*CP*, 180).

"Blue Guitar" reaches its next crisis and probably its resolution in part 30. The poverty of the contemporary cannot be healed, and the poet must accept this reality as his subject and substance. Two images that merge and separate throughout the series, the theater and the natural scene, join in his final portrait of the poet:

> From this I shall evolve a man.
> This is his essence: the old fantoche
>
> Hanging his shawl upon the wind,
> Like something on the stage, puffed out. . . . (*CP*, 181)

An entertainer less in control than the juggler, the *fantoche* or marionette is yet a man, an apposite spokesman for the truth that "Oxidia is Olympia": the reality on which poetry must be based is the depressingly mechanized, uninspired present. This conclusion reached, the last few sections of the poem build on the acceptance of Oxidia as Olympia. The question now seems to be, Is poetry even possible? In part 31, the poet is relegated to a seedy workaday world, where "The employer and employee contend, / Combat, compose their droll affair." This is no place for the traditional romantic: "There is no place, / Here, for the lark fixed in the mind." The music of this time cannot be "fixed," and it must be "the rhapsody of things as they are." Still, in this time as in all eras poetry must be possible, and a few instructions follow in part 32. Basic directives for a poetry of impoverishment, they involve a purification, a stripping away of accretions:

> Throw away the lights, the definitions,
> And say of what you see in the dark
> That it is this or that it is that,
> But do not use the rotted names. (*CP*, 183)

The "crust of shape" has been destroyed, allowing the self and the world a certain freedom and a time for reinvigoration and renaming.

The last section reaches again toward affirmation, although it is a sharply limited and qualified affirmation. Poetry based on actuality can be redemptive. The dream of the generation is "aviled / In the mud, in Monday's dirty light" (*CP*, 183). One must live in the present, accepting the bread and stone that are its elements. A parallel with the bread and wine of the eucharist is suggested, but this communion is a form of participation in the earth; one takes in the natural in a secular sacrament, and this sacred meal renews the bond with nature. In the daylight world of the ordinary, one lives without poetry. Nevertheless, there are times when one chooses "to play / The imagined pine, the imagined jay" (*CP*, 184). It is the nature of the poet to create, and thus to redeem, his world and renew it. The conclusion is a return from imaginative possibility to the limitations of reality.

The poem that follows, "A Thought Revolved," can be seen as a coda to the long poem that precedes it. Its three parts explore ways of substituting reality for metaphysics. The "lady dying of diabetes" in part 1, the "Mechanical Optimist," allows the canned reassurances of the radio to lead her gently out of life. She is already dead to the life of the mind; too much sugar has rendered her comatose. Part 2, "Mystic Garden & Middling Beast," describes "the poet striding among cigar stores" who actively chronicles the real as he sees it and participates in it. This is the vulgarized and barren society of Oxidia, but the poet is awakened and challenged by its difficulty. Part 3, "Romanesque Affabulation" (to "affabulate" is to turn to legend or myth), describes the poet's search for a father-leader figure based on the human, not on some concept of divinity. This godless earth needs a human legend, a legend that concentrates the essence of humanity into a symbolic figure. Part 4 posits the creation of such a hero, but it is an obscure and difficult imaginative exercise, producing an ambiguous, unsatisfactory result. This poem, like the last, seeks to anchor the poetic in the flux of daily experience and to show the revitalizing effects of energetic imagining. It represents a cycle, from the death of one myth through the inception and definition of another, which will ultimately prove to be as unsatisfying as the first.

Ideas of Order, *Owl's Clover*, and *The Man with the Blue Guitar* show Stevens's attempts to engage the contemporary, and *The Man with the Blue Guitar* begins to chronicle his developing preoccupation with the poet-hero who will not, like Hoon, create a world from the contents of his mind but instead will construct a poetry of "things as they are." In their ongoing struggle with the antipoetic, Stevens's poems show a progression through the effete disgust of some of the earliest poems and the argumentative confrontation of *Owl's Clover* toward an acceptance of the surface of the ordinary as the substance of poetry—one might say toward a materialist poetic. But the argument of "The Man with the Blue Guitar" may be unconvincing to the reader. "The imagined pine, the imagined jay"—the most ordinary of the ordinary, however reenvisioned—are unsatisfactory compensation for the spiritual poverty endemic to the modern world. That his argument did not convince the poet either is evident from the direction taken by the following books.

It is of interest that the time period spanned by *Ideas of Order*, *Owl's Clover*, and *The Man with the Blue Guitar* saw the intensification of Stevens's famous proxy shopping expeditions, rendered famous by Frank Lentriccia's discussion of them in *Ariel and the Police* (1988).[6] Stevens some years earlier had begun asking his far-flung correspondents to send him surprise packages that would provide him with the spirit of a place he had never visited. He seemed to be asking friends to bring him place, to deliver the lares and penates of other dwellings, just as later, in the throes of an absorbing interest in genealogy, he would be asking others to bring him time, bring him history, his own and that of his region. His shopping expeditions are another instance of his attempt to create new sacraments in which the actual is invested with the spiritual. In his poetry, he attempted to define a poetic that would rest on the tangible, like the Buddha received in the mail that for him came to represent Ceylon.[7]

Chapter Four

"This Descant of a Self":
Parts of a World

In 1942 Stevens published *Parts of a World*, a tentative, explorative book, and also the limited Cummington Press edition of *Notes toward a Supreme Fiction*, both of which show the beginnings of his "edgings and inchings toward final form" (*CP*, 488). In these works, metaphysical concerns resurface as Stevens attempts to define a credible hero. The human, as it turns out, is not quite firm enough ground on which to base a credo. *Parts of a World* can be seen as a commentary on "Notes toward a Supreme Fiction" (to be discussed as part of the book *Transport to Summer*), but both 1942 books represent attempts to rebuild on the bare foundations of the stripped aesthetic.

If critics in the 1930s challenged Stevens's poetics, the turmoil of the 1940s posed a more subtle threat. The international tensions that culminated in war, as well as unexpected deaths in Stevens's family, might have produced a retreat back into the aestheticism of *Harmonium* or even into silence. But Stevens's reaction was unexpected. The element of nostalgia for lost forms, always present in Stevens, is minimal in the collection *Parts of a World*. Instead, the poems have an affirmative motion, and it is in this collection particularly that the famous Stevens "as if" makes its presence strongly felt. The book begins on a note of jubilance that sparkles through the poems, and even the long, meditative "Examination of the Hero in Time of War" at the end of the book concludes positively. The poet had found a perspective that was satisfying and, "for a moment, final" (*CP*, 168).

Stevens's reaction to the exigencies of an increasingly ugly contemporary world was, as he expressed it in an essay delivered at Princeton, to press back with the imagination. Such an act reasserted humanistic values in a time of chaos, making poetry a social force without turning it into social poetry and identifying poetry with action. The hero figure that had begun to evolve in his last two books began to assume various specific forms, especially that of the soldier. The compromise position taken in "Men That Are Falling"—that individuals die in and for an ideal and that this ideal gives meaning to their deaths—may have seemed romantic and sentimental to the 1940s Stevens. In fact, much of his early work may have seemed to him a vast oversimplification that was not appropriate to the complexity of a confusing and iconless present. He read others' accounts of their attempts to link poetry and society. His readings in the late 1930s and early 1940s included Benedetto Croce's *Defense of Poetry* (1933), Giambattista Vico's *New Science* (1725–44), Rainer Maria Rilke's *Letters to a Young Poet* (1929), and other literary and philosophical works whose common theme is the primary value of poetry, which he found to be transformative and even redemptive (Richardson II, 171).

In working out his justification for poetry, Stevens found that the catastrophe of war forced him to redefine his aesthetic. In his reassessment, the transcendent, more or less banished in *The Man with the Blue Guitar*, reasserts itself as the sanction for poetry and for other heroic activity. Perhaps personal and national insecurities also spurred his developing interest in genealogy, an interest that began about 1939 and occupied him for more than ten years. The deaths of friends and family members, especially his brother John's death in 1940, spurred him to scan the traces left by his family on history; Elsie, too, who was also losing family members to death, became involved in charting her family lines. Genealogy was one of the few interests the couple pursued together. They enjoyed sharing over the dinner table the progress they had made in uncovering family lines; these discoveries broke the usual silence.

Holly Stevens reports that her father's interest in genealogical researches was intense in the years surrounding 1942 (*LWS*, 397). His letters show that tracing his family lines became something of an obsession with him, rivaling his passion for acquiring foreign images in the form of artifacts and paintings. During this era, the past becomes personalized in his poems, identified with individual Dutch ancestors.

Stevens's preoccupation with genealogy was a way of dissipating the nostalgia and feelings of loss that always affected him; it allowed him to take hold of the past. Comforting relationships that seemed easily accessible to others eluded him. His early poems show his sense that he was too late for traditional religion; it comforted his mother and informed her life, but it could not do so for him. In a sense, he also missed out on family intimacy. He had quarreled with his father over Elsie and was never reconciled. He had not since childhood been very close with his siblings, and now all but one were dead. His youngest sister, Mary Katherine, had died in the war in 1919; her war letters show a gift for writing as well as a passionate commitment to justice.[1] Her early death briefly reawakened Stevens's interest in family things (*LWS*, 212–14), but his attention soon turned back to business. Stevens's two brothers, Garrett Barcalow Stevens and John Bergen Stevens, died in 1937 and 1940, respectively. When he was finishing the poems of *Parts of a World*, there remained of the original family only Wallace and his sister Elizabeth Stevens MacFarland, with whom he occasionally corresponded about family matters. Stevens's relationships with his wife and daughter were certainly not intimate; Elsie and Wallace spoke very little to one another, even when Holly was present with guests, and after a silent, ritual family dinner, both spouses fled to their private quarters. Stevens became more reminiscent and nostalgic in his letters about his family; in a letter to his remaining sister shortly before she died, he commiserated with her about her daughter's unwillingness to do what she wanted, noting that Holly too seemed out of control, and then looked back at his own youth: "I felt exactly the same way when I was her age; I took the family for granted" (*LWS*, 421). Now that the family was almost gone, he realized its value—and yet it would seem from the infrequency and casual tone of his letters to Elizabeth that he still took her for granted. Only after the generation was completely gone did he reach out after its traces.

Instead of his real family, it would seem that Stevens invested himself in the abstract idea of family, of spiritual connections. He did try to keep up somewhat with the younger members of the family, his brothers' and sister's children, but had a difficult time of it, partly owing to his natural reticence. All human communication seemed to him flawed and incomplete, but the poetry of *Parts of a World* and *Transport to Summer* expresses an intense desire for true communication, or communion, and sometimes uses images of the family in an attempt to portray a potential fulfillment. With both religion and the family, it would seem that Stevens first, partly through his own diffidence, rejected or withdrew from home and church; then was no longer able to connect; then missed the association acutely; and finally substituted a figurative or abstract concept of the relationship with church and with family that he had been unable to maintain when each was present as a reality. These abstract concepts begin to coalesce into an idea of "home," a spiritual foyer that is far from any of Stevens's actual homes. In these two books, there is an upward and outward motion as Stevens rejoices in this ability to abstract, to create a myth based on the present but not limited to its time-bound particulars, and to note how this myth is fed by the past and feeds the future.

The collection *Parts of a World* reflects Stevens's attempt to locate himself in history as well as to explain or justify poetry in time of war. Its analysis of the hero and of the poetic act as a heroic effort that had meaning even in wartime shows his continued concern with the issues raised for him by the leftist critics of the 1930s. If the depression and international tensions had outdated traditional art, they sparked the search for artistic renewal, which was Stevens's consistent focus. Since the old, ordered world was gone forever, so were the premises of its art. The question that pursued Stevens into the 1940s was, Is not poetry self-serving and escapist? He answered the challenge in both poetry and essay by claiming that poetry is not self-serving; it serves humankind. It is indeed escapist, but its escapism is a virtue rather than a fault. The escape offered by poetry is transcendence rather than evasion and provides a chance for renewing and refreshing reality by reenvisioning it. Thus, these poems contain less elegy and more hope. They are not argumentative in a prosaic sense (like the poems of *Owl's Clover*), but they do present and affirm an aesthetic through image and metaphor.

"The Noble Rider and the Sound of Words," written at the beginning of l941 and read at Princeton in May of that year, expresses Stevens's difficulties in defining the poet's role for his time, while it also continues the debate, begun in the 1930s, over the poet's social responsibility. The essay traces the unequal and shifting balance between reality and imagination throughout various eras and places, concluding that at present reality represents an overwhelming force that it is the poet's duty to resist, not by falsifying but by pressing back with the imagination. The essay elaborates on ideas first presented in "The Irrational Element in Poetry," but the Princeton lecture is more focused and incisive. "The idea of nobility exists in art today only in degenerate forms or in a much diminished state, if, in fact, it exists at all," Stevens observes. "This is due to failure in the relation between the imagination and reality."[2]

He explains that the pressure of reality has caused the failure. The poet-hero, heir of Plato in a dissolute time, must press back against reality with the imagination. His role is "to help people live their lives"; to do this, he will address an elite, "not . . . a drab but . . . a woman with the hair of a pythoness" (*NA*, 29). The world's violence and the urgency of its encounters must be reflected in its fictions. (The pythoness, incidentally, is not a Gorgon but a prophetess, a priestess of Apollo.) By finding the right words, by using the sounds of words acutely, the poet will restructure experience. The address concludes, "The mind has added nothing to human nature. It is a violence from within that protects us from a violence without. It is the imagination pressing back against the pressure of reality. It seems, in the last analysis, to have something to do with our self-preservation; and that, no doubt, is why the expression of it, the sound of its words, helps us to live our lives" (*NA*, 36). Naturally and appropriately, violent events in the world evoke a violent response in the mind. The mind and the world are worthy opponents in an ongoing struggle to determine which will prevail.

Stevens was writing this essay while he finished *Parts of a World*, and the new collection shows the application of his premises. These poems reflect the intensification of his belief that poetry is action, not merely meditation—that the act of poetry is heroic. They also continue his earlier trends. Once again, he insists that creating verse is not for romantic escapists but rather is the essence of total involvement in one's time and place. The notion of the poet-hero takes on clearer definition, but the focus of Stevens's attention is not only on the hero himself but on the act of creation. Poetry is never static; the poet is continually, fully involved in the decreation that results in renewed and renewing perception.

These poems, like the essay, also develop Stevens's unique sense of place as central to poetry, establishing place as part of the dynamic of the interaction between mind and world. "Place" is time as well as location, and it consists of all the sensory observations that constitute the experience. "One is not duchess / A hundred yards from a carriage," he noted in *Harmonium* (*CP*, 86), and not ten minutes away from one either. Individual identity is a complex matrix in which the conscious self is inextricably linked to the specifics of one's location in time and space— one's "weather." The interior world reflects the texture of the exterior.

There remains for Stevens, however, a division between self and weather that cannot be bridged. That distance is the "belatedness" involved in the act of perception. The poet is always "behind"; he never manages to catch up with the present. The attempt to break through the tissue that separates the thing from the conception of the thing, the reality from its interpreted form, is what makes poetry. To engage reality is an energetic activity that demands full involvement, as Stevens insisted repeatedly in both prose and poetry. This effort to efface the "belatedness" so that the perceived is identified with the real is the core of the poetic act. It is an act of faith.

The poems of *Parts of a World* are less sensuous and concrete than those of *Harmonium* and *Ideas of Order*, but they continue the meditative strain that appears in *Owl's Clover* and later poems. The image density of these poems diminishes, and the pictorial content is rarely the poem's center. The images in this collection are often truncated and elided, sometimes suddenly abandoned to communicate the feeling of poetry as act, making the poem itself an action. These poems circle around the poetic process, approaching it through metaphors of creation and change. The evolution of the human being is the process in "On an Old Horn," which describes through images of evolution the achievement of realizing full humanity and finding one's voice to articulate the fiction of self. Other poems consider the plastic arts, natural transformations, and common human activities as processes analogous to, as well as instances of, the poetic act. The idea of poetry as action, as the expenditure of energy in an attempt to master, is the central focus of this collection. Reading *Parts of a World* as part of *The Collected Poems* may give the impression that Stevens had speeded up the pace of his poems and rigorously cut away the deadweight of anything that could be considered passive. These poems are smooth and swift.

Parts of a World gives a theory and a practice of a poetics that is a kind of alchemy. Stevens has always used images of the sacraments of Christianity to describe creative perception; this equation is an important part of "The Man with the Blue Guitar." In "Blue Guitar," however, the separation of vehicle and tenor is clear, and the sacraments are clearly symbols of the elements of creative perception. In the poems of *Parts of a World*, the transformative processes of the mystical-magical sacred study blur into the definitions of poetic creation; poetry *is* alchemy. As in alchemy, the self is refined and purified, and as a result, the process also renews and clarifies itself. The first part of this collection is more theoretical and tends to be filled with caveats and imperatives. The second part is more illustrative, with concrete examples of the alembic in full boil.[3]

Patchwork, pieces, irrelevancies, are hallmarks of this collection. "The Man on the Dump" is a direct and clear statement of the poet's predicament. The dump is a cosmic wasteland where all the things of daily life that time brings into disuse pile up. Everything, however exotic or ordinary, eventually ends up here:

> . . . the janitor's poems
> Of every day, the wrapper on the can of pears,
> The cat in the paper-bag, the corset, the box
> From Esthonia: the tiger chest, for tea. (*CP*, 201)

This is the cosmic dump from *Owl's Clover* again, but reimagined in a more positive light. The useless miscellany of the dump at first engenders Stevens's standard speculations about transience: "How many women have covered themselves / With dew, dew dresses, stones and chains of dew." But in addition to evanescence and impermanence, the dew also suggests freshness and immediacy, and the mood shifts abruptly to the positive element. Although it is ironic that men and women should mistake dew for permanent adornment, change is good. "One feels the purifying change. One rejects / the trash" (*CP*, 202). As in "Sunday Morning," death is the mother of beauty. But unlike in the earlier poem, here the emphasis is not on passive acceptance, a letting go of myth and yielding to the natural cycle, but on active participation in the relentless principle of renewal. The mind struggles to divest itself of its prisons, to see things in the light of their naked truth:

> . . . the moon comes up as the moon
> (All its images are in the dump) and you see
> As a man (not like an image of a man),
> You see the moon rise in the empty sky. (*CP*, 202)

The discards are canceled images, sheddings of past perceptions. Stevens's later poems are filled with references to such husks, necessary sacrifices to revitalization.

Given that the dump is reality, what is left? Desire is left, desire for a credo based on the actual and inherent in it:

> One sits and beats an old tin can, lard pail.
> One beats and beats for that which one believes.
> That's what one wants to get near. Could it after all
> Be merely oneself . . . ? (*CP*, 202)

What is left is the examining, desiring self. The poem asks, Is the self the myth we seek? The nightingale, symbol of the romantic, has its falseness become so obvious that it can only be an annoyance, like an old scratched phonograph record? Perhaps the whole flock of birds/poets are not the true "solace" the ear seeks, for desire is too deep for any accessible consolation. It is an itch beneath the skin.[4]

The series of questions at the conclusion may be interpreted as one: Is the poetic act redemptive? The last line of the poem merges question and statement: "Where was it one first heard of the truth? The the." The line has been read as a suggestion that there is no "the," no definite article, and hence no definition. Other readings include the identification of "the the" with the stripped world, "the irreducible minimum" (Litz,

262). But the query of the man on the dump may suggest that the whole activity of casting off is a search for "the the," an attempt to hunt the undistorted real back to its source. This poem may have been suggested by a real hermit Stevens had observed living on a dump not far from his home, a man who projected an evocative image of enforced asceticism (Richardson II, 92). The hermit, believed to be a Russian refugee, had built a shelter from the castoffs and lived there for years. Stevens's speaker in "Man on the Dump" also in a sense constructs a life from the discards of time and meditates on the truths that the dump reveals.

"Man and Bottle," another poem about the confrontation between desire and actuality, illustrates the mind's necessary but always ultimately unsatisfactory engagement with reality. Mind and man are "the great poem of winter," recalling the frozen spectator, the Snow Man. To "find what will suffice," the mind "destroys romantic tenements / Of rose and ice." Just as "Sailing after Lunch" calls for the abolition and the renewal of the romantic, such that it is always in the process of becoming, this poem describes decreation as a necessary part of discovery. Moreover, this current scene is "the land of war," and war itself must be fitted into any imaginative system. Like imaginative decreation, war must be considered a destruction of old orders. Thus, war has a teleological function to its destructiveness.

When the force of reality is compared with the force of the mind, however, it is the force of the mind that wins out. Inner weather dominates:

> It is not the snow that is the quill, the page.
> The poem lashes more fiercely than the wind,
> As the mind, to find what will suffice, destroys
> Romantic tenements of rose and ice. (*CP*, 238)

The phrase "rose and ice" suggests a blending, an accommodation, between the imagined and the real, but not a lasting one. The romantic must neither endure nor remain, as the speaker explains in "Sailing after Lunch." Yet its impetus, the desire for the transcendent, underlies all art. The poet is the thinker whose fierce purity of thought refuses to accept compromises. Yet he or she must continue to search for "what will suffice"—a goal articulated in the same words in other poems, including the frequently anthologized "Of Modern Poetry" (which will be discussed later). The goal of art is a mind-world relationship that will provide the same kind of sustenance as the great belief systems of the past.

"Asides on the Oboe" is an important poem in this volume for what it adds to Stevens's definition of the concept of the hero. (More than any other of Stevens's collections, *Parts of a World* is about the hero.) "The prologues are over," the poem begins; the mythologies of the past, which were believed to hold absolute truth, have been collectively dismissed. The idea that there could be such a truth has been dismissed: "the final belief / Must be in a fiction" (*CP*, 250). This passage encapsulates the theme of Stevens's middle period. He was preoccupied with the "fiction" itself, and with the university chair of poetry he hoped to establish through the generosity of his friend Henry Church. (He had the notion of establishing something like the Charles Eliot Norton Chair at Harvard. He hoped to create in this way a major pulpit for the strongest poetic voices of the period.) But as his search for the ultimate fiction and its priests continued, it would seem that imagination took the place of the individual poet, and the chair became an abstraction too exalted for human occupancy. In "The Auroras of Autumn," he asks: "Is there an imagination that sits enthroned / As grim as it is benevolent?" (*CP*, 417)

In "Asides on the Oboe," the fictions of the past, the gods killed by Boucher (the anthropologist presumably, not the artist), and the human heroes ("the metal heroes that time granulates") are obsolete. Only "the impossible possible philosophers' man," the alchemist-thinker, is still in the present, "still walks in dew" (*CP*, 251). The dew has the same suggestions it has in "Sunday Morning" on the feet of the sun worshipers. It indicates that the hero is so in tune with reality that he can touch time in its passage. He is the "central man" who as a "human globe" both reflects and interprets the human situation. Alchemical imagery controls the poem. The central man is a quintessence, a philosopher's stone, but in Stevens's words in a different context, he is "a thinking stone" (*CP*, 13). He is person blended with place, a literal microcosm. He creates by naming: "Thou art not August unless I make thee so" (*CP*, 251).

The poem then shifts to the war, where "the jasmine islands were bloody martyrdoms": violent events transformed beauty to horror. What good was the poet then, the speaker asks: "How was it then with the central man? Did we / Find peace?" (*CP*, 251). The answer is that the central man reflected and interpreted this too, so that we at least had the peace of being at one with ourselves and our time and place. His song for the fallen makes human life bearable by investing it with meaning, even though this meaning is dependent on accidental contingencies. We know ourselves through him, not through an "external reference" like the Christian God or some other "external" entity.

> . . . we were wholly one, as we heard
> Him chanting for those buried in their blood,
> In the jasmine haunted forests, that we knew
> The glass man, without external reference. (*CP*, 251)

The glass man is one manifestation of the hero. This is the way the poet helps "men live their lives": by articulating the nobility of their lives, the potential and actual nobility of humankind. The glass man is microcosm to the diamond globe. Self-knowledge becomes knowledge of the world, and vice versa. It is not the case, as in Stevens's earlier poems about soldiers dying, that men die in and for an ideal that ennobles their deaths. It is more that this way of dying is an essentially human event, and that in mourning for these deaths—expressing grief in song and story, "chanting" the memorial of lives lost—the true nature of our being is manifested.

But if interpretation can provide freedom, it can also, of course, confine. Freedom from the prisons of interpretations is a major theme of this collection, explored in "On the Road Home," "The Latest Freed Man," and other poems. Liberation results from the active purification of perception; the strenuous, disciplined mental act is poetry. The act is both creative and destructive; in uncovering and discovering, it also imposes, thereby falsifying. Thus, every creative act, as Stevens insisted from the beginning, is both a revelation and violation of reality. "Add This to Rhetoric" explores the irony of rhetoric's dual nature: "It is posed and it is posed, / But in nature it merely grows" (*CP*, 198). The artificiality is not only in the choice of words but in the perception itself. Once more, Stevens describes how the actual outlasts and diminishes all representations of it. The one reality, the sun, is beyond all attempts to describe it; it "comes up as the sun," yesterday's images having left "no shadows of themselves." Yet this imaging persists, and it is the act of perception itself, not merely the will, that determines it: "The sense creates the pose" (*CP*, 199). There is no way around the fact that even vision is a lie, or partial truth at most.

The problematical reciprocity between mind and world is more fully expounded in "Connoisseur of Chaos," a poem that explores, again with Stevens's ironic distancing, the peculiar paradox that

> A. A violent order is disorder; and
> B. A great disorder is an order. These
> Two things are one. (Pages of illustrations.) (*CP*, 215)

The imposition of order on nature is a violation; however, order comes from the mind, because it is the nature of the mind to perceive it. We cannot go back to the old order, the time "when bishops' books / Resolved the world," because reality is not controllable by these old interpretations or by any rigid structure. Rather, "The squirming facts exceed the squamous mind" (*CP*, 215). Still, elements of relation are perceived. Truths are all separate propositions, including the truth that order is disorder. This is "just one more truth, one more / Element in the immense disorder of truths." Stevens's notion of chaos parallels the interpretations of the chaos theorist James Gleick, who finds patterns and shapes in chaos.[5] The poem speculates: "Suppose the disorder of truths should ever come / To an order, most Plantagenet, most fixed" (*CP*, 216). A Plantagenet order, the analogical universe with everything in its place in the Great Chain of Being is presented as a remote possibility, to be approached no more closely than by a cautious ellipsis. The use of "Plantagenet" as an adjective also provides an ironic distancing. Yet when Stevens invites us to suppose something, he is requesting that this possibility be entertained and its consequences imagined. The possibility of an unknown cosmic order is left distantly open.

The two statements of the poem therefore are one: at the extreme, order is disorder, disorder is order. The poem then shifts to the vision that has produced this insight, that of "the pensive man" who "sees that eagle float / For which the intricate Alps are a single nest" (*CP*, 216). The pensive man's perspective is not the same as that of the eagle, for the man remains earthbound, but his informed vision allows him to imagine what the eagle sees: an overview that finds the pattern in chaos and, moreover, finds that very form/formlessness to be home—the eagle's own nest. Stevens here approaches an abstract theism.

That the poetic quest gives pleasure is a given. "Parochial Theme" captures the feeling of exhilarating change as it describes hunters in the pines and exults in the vitality and immediacy of their hunting: "This health is holy, this descant of a self, / This barbarous chanting of what is strong, this blare" (*CP*, 191). Poetry = participation = the act of hunting, the frenzied pursuit and the shouts of discovery. But then the poem asks once more the persistent question of "Sunday Morning": "Where, then, is paradise?" "Parochial Theme" asks, What does it do to the hope of permanence to invest fully in the present? "But salvation here? What about the rattle of sticks / On tins and boxes? What about horses eaten by wind?" (*CP*, 191). The answer to the need for some "imperishable bliss" is the same and yet different from that of the earlier poem.

> Health follows after health. Salvation there:
> There's no such thing as life, or if there is
> It is faster than the weather. . . . (*CP*, 192)

Here the meditator is not advised to yield to transience as a good and accept death as the mother of beauty but rather is exhorted to take action, to allow his or her own energy to be part of the pulse of energy that is life, whatever that is. It is necessary to work to perceive within the flux of things, find whatever order is to be invented or discovered: "Piece the world together, boys, but not with your hands." That is, assemble it with your eye, with your unique sensibility, the poet is saying through this sudden, ebullient shift of person. He tells the "boys" that they should not merely build an arbitrary order for the world. The sensibility, purified by its total immersion in the act of discovering, is rewarded by a vital perception that finds the order in disorder. Like the eagle, this educated sentience is able to interpret "the intricate Alps" as "a single nest"; from its height it can approximate a divine overview.

Stevens's use of hunting as a trope for poetry is unusual for him. But the hunter metaphor emphasizes the energetic pursuit and the finding aspect of poetry, in contrast to some of his earlier figures for the imagination; moreover, the hunters are male, stereotypically so. Their sounds are the halloos of discovery and communication, and they are incipient, nonfinal: "the voices / Have shapes that are not yet fully themselves" (*CP*, 190). The total involvement in the hunt is a "health," and the formless energy of the search takes the form of a self-assertion. The "descant of a self" and the "barbarous chanting" bring to mind Whitman's "barbaric yawp" that he sounds "over the roofs of the world." And yet Stevens's hunters' cry suggests more selection, more discipline, and more control than Whitman's "barbaric yawp": the relationship between mind and world, self and other, is more rigorously defined. "Song of Myself" asserts, "I depart as air . . . I effuse my flesh in eddies";[6] in the Stevens poem, the identification of self and flux is so strong that dissolution into sheer being becomes a real possibility. Stevens's reading of Heidegger and Husserl may inform this breathless vision of the disappearance of presence into pure potency: "There's no such thing as life; or if there is, / It is faster than the weather" (*CP*, 192).

"Dezembrum" is another poem of renewal that, like "Parochial Theme," expresses joy in the revitalized reenvisionings that follow conclusions. Its five unrhymed quatrains describe the process of renewal and the motive for poetry. The past configurations of the cosmos are swept away, like the old constellations and the stories of debunked gods:

> The sky is no longer a junk-shop,
> Full of javelins and old fire-balls,
> Triangles and the names of girls. (*CP*, 218)

There are only "the winter stars" now; endings are strippings. The function of the year's end is to empty the sky of "junk" and leave it a blank slate for the future's scribblings.

The second section considers the genesis of godhead and how the world divides itself into man and "imagined man" or "god." One projects the imagined self onto the screen of the sky. Parts 3 and 4 describe the celestial scene as human now, reflecting what humankind needs most—friendship, song, and laughter, not angels or messages from the dead. Part 5 focuses on the reciprocal relationship between the meditator and the winter sky. The sky reflects his need, he is fulfilled. He can read love out of the sky instead of someone else's interpretations—the old gods, the junk-shop "thing-a-ma-jigs." The last two lines are a blunt summary: "The reason can give nothing at all / like the response to desire" (*CP*, 218). It is human desire and human need that people the skies. This is a joyful peopling and repeopling that can never come to closure, and never should. "Dezembrum" asserts the need for gods but skirts the issue of whether this need comes ultimately from the mind or from the sky. More and more the poems suggest that the need, or desire, for divinity is sanctioned.

The activity of stripping is distanced and objectified in "Landscape with Boat." The title suggests a painting in which the boat is a focal point ordering the landscape, much like the jar in "Anecdote of the Jar." The "anti-master man" of the first line is described as a "floribund ascetic." The phrase is an oxymoron, since "floribund" ordinarily describes roses bearing copious blooms and seems a surprising modifier for "ascetic." But the combination suggests the impossibility of the quest as well as its nature. What the seeker wants is the world completely true—reduced to itself, with no imaginative projections upon it. He "looked for the world beneath the blue / without blue, without any turquoise hint or phase" (*CP*, 241). His goal: uninterpreted reality. But the ascetic is wrongheaded in his quest. In his search for "the neutral centre, the ominous element," he overlooks the fact that his creating/ perceiving self might be a "truth, himself, or part of it." The world without the imagination is "single-colored, colorless"; the imagination colors the world by giving it its tones of blue. But the imagination itself is as much a part of reality as the world it interprets, so that the blueness is an integral part of the system, not a falsification of it. The realization of the inevitable immanence of blue might bring the ascetic back to the green of reality, but with his perceptive abilities sharpened so as to draw from the real its essence,

> He might sit on a sofa on a balcony
> Above the Mediterranean, emerald
> Becoming emeralds. (*CP*, 243)

He would be able to reify reality, to watch its abstractions assume concrete form. His new awareness might bring him to the epiphany that he is in tune with the universe, that the song he is singing is the one that is there for him to sing. "The thing I hum appears to be / The rhythm of this celestial pantomime" (*CP*, 243). If we accept the "floribund ascetic" as straightforward rather than ironic, the poem also concludes with a theistic perspective. The artist behind the "celestial pantomime" whose rhythms could be picked up by an open-minded seeker is assumed to be present, at least in the conditional.

"Extracts from Addresses to the Academy of Fine Ideas" shares with "Examination of the Hero in Time of War" the themes of the soldier-hero as exemplar and the need for poetry in times of extremity, and a theistic determination lurks in both. "Extracts" links the soldier image to the explanation of evil and pain that Stevens would develop more fully in "Esthétique du Mal." The poem consists of eight sections of unequal numbers of lines of loose iambic pentameter; one section has its lines arranged as couplets. The title "Extracts from Addresses to the Academy of Fine Ideas" undercuts the poem; Stevens's quirky self-irony may confuse. If these are only extracts from dry academic addresses, how seriously are we to take them? The speaker addresses his listeners as "Messieurs," confirming the impression. Yet the tone of condescension and superiority does not obviate the speaker's desire for clarity, for reality. The world of the literary consists of paper roses that "make a brilliant sound"; the noises "pelt" an ear of glass. The listener is invited to

> Compare the silent rose of the sun
> And rain, the blood-rose living in its smell
> With this paper, this dust. (*CP*, 252)

The speaker would like a world safe for the Academy of Fine Ideas, but there is no such world, except on paper. Reality is too powerful for us, he claims, at least for those of us who address the Academy. We have to live in a paper world in which "the false and the true are one." Thus, part 1 introduces a reality too strong and dangerous for "fine ideas" and presents an Academy spokesman who is trying to grapple with the problem.

Part 2 takes up the problem of attempting to explain the evil in such a world. The speaker, who seems to be the same as in part 1, addresses his listeners as "my beards," fellow cognoscenti in an artificial world. He pontificates to the effect that evil can be perceived aesthetically. It can be explained away in the context of a good system; it can be "glazed."

> Evil made magic, as in catastrophe
> if neatly glazed, becomes the same as the fruit
> of an emperor, the egg-plant of a prince. (*CP*, 253)

Neatly glazing evil may be the Pangloss solution of assuming any specific evil must have some good effects, somehow, somewhere. Perhaps Stevens thought the critics had accused him of such glazing or glossing; some of his earlier poems are certainly open to such accusation. Clearly, this solution is not satisfactory. The speaker wishes to set up a contrast, a distinction, between "evil death" and "good death." The "good death" may be a death that can, on some unexplained grounds, be acceptable, perhaps because it happens as part of the natural cycle of seasons, whereas "evil death" may be more akin to the arbitrarily imposed slaughter of wartime. The speaker seems to be playing with ideas in parts 1 and 2, asserting and then discarding them amid a papery company that, like himself, is isolated from the real world, the "blood-rose living in its smell."

The professor figure seems to disappear at the end of part 2. Part 3 may be seen as a commentary on the professor-rhetorician of parts 1 and 2. It looks at the proposition that "all men are priests." Priesthood was confined to a few "lean cats of the arches of the churches" in the old world, but now each man is an evangelist. The plethora of positions results in fragmentation and trivialization of thought. At least the "lean cats" who were preachers of the old world had "a sense of their design," a reason and justification to "savor the sunlight." Part 4 represents a feeble attempt by one who has experienced the chill of winter to reorient himself to his landscape, redefine himself in a place that has undergone the change of seasons. So far, the direction of the poem is from the artificial toward the real.

The next section takes up the notion of "seasons of belief," the rise and fall of ideologies. This section alone is in couplets, perhaps suggesting thesis and antithesis by the form. The conflict between ideas is in fact represented as a gunfight, in which

> philosophical assassins pull
> Revolvers and shoot each other. One remains.
>
> The mass of meaning becomes composed again. (*CP*, 256)

The triumphant assassin "sings in chaos," for the moment victorious. Part 6 shifts to the image of Hercules, "Ercole," who may represent the earth-self. The mind-self is "that other one" who wanted to "think his way to life, / Sure that the ultimate poem was the mind" (*CP*, 256). The solution is not a simple compromise—"It cannot be half earth, half mind; half sun, / Half thinking" (*CP*, 257). The meditated solution, the "redeeming thought" or the fiction has to satisfy the mind.

Parts 7 and 8 are parallel explorations of this solacing fiction, part 7 discussing its happy implications and part 8 its unhappy ones. Part 7 celebrates the "ecstatic identities / Between one's self and the weather" that are possible in a world without illusion. Part 8 tries to answer once more the request for "imperishable bliss" in "Sunday Morning," here put in the form of a query: If we strip the illusions from war, then what are the soldiers dying for? How can we even sing their praises?

> How can
> We chant if we live in evil and afterward
> Lie harshly buried there? (*CP*, 259)

The question is important enough to be separated out from the rest of the poem. The answer is obscure. It seems that if nothing is final, evil is also "dissolved," in life as well as in death. It is the poet's job to find the ultimate words for this resolution, in the "heart's residuum." He or she must find "a single line, equal to memory," that perhaps has the power of redeeming life—"one line in which / The vital music formulates the words" (*CP*, 259).

This poem starts with the clutter of ideas that are tossed about the wordy academy and proceeds to the assertion of the possibility of the single line "equal to memory." In its explorations, it analyzes the foundations of fiction, the means by which ideologies or fictions come to dominate, and the power of fiction to serve as a narrative elegy. The poem is difficult to follow because of the blurring of voices and masks and the not-unusual problem of identifying which is the poem's true voice. The line "equal to memory," however, remains a tantalizing concept: the desire, envisioned as a distant possibility, to truly immortalize in poetry not merely the beloved's image but the sentient being itself.

Parts of a World takes steps toward the supreme fiction, toward that realization of what the sun worshipers in "Sunday Morning" might finally represent. The energetic activity of stripping reality is followed by a kind of grace, a re-perception of reality that is enlightenment. This comes of itself and is nothing permanent. It involves a participation in reality that is a reward for the hero, the poet-hero who becomes a stronger presence as the poetry proceeds. The long poem "Montrachet-le-Jardin" explores this ideal as it is so far posited.

The poem begins with a farewell to the kind of certainty achieved at the end of "Sunday Morning." The pleasures of the senses are not enough. What, then, is? Sensory perceptions, such as the taste of a glass of Montrachet-le-Jardin, are particulars of something underneath, that life or being that is "faster than the weather" in the collection's opening poem. The truth of being is seen as a message, articulated by the hero although inherent in nature.

> To-night, night's undeciphered murmuring
> Comes close to the prisoner's ear, becomes a throat
> The hand can touch, neither green bronze or marble,
> The hero's throat in which the words are spoken. . . . (*CP*, 261)

Words are blended with feeling in a message that is a complete communication, "a throat / The hand can touch." The reaching out is both physical and intellectual. Senses melt into each other in a complete understanding that is at once intuitive, sensuous, and verbal.

The main burden of the poem is that "Man must become the hero of his world." To do this, he must become stripped, naked: "the naked man as last / And tallest hero and plus gaudiest vir" (*CP*, 262). The "naked

man"/"gaudiest vir" contrast parallels the "floribund ascetic" of
"Landscape with Boat"; the two parallels help to explicate each other.
There is a point at which stripping is adornment, and "naked" is then
"gaudiest." The hero delineated by this poem is not clearly defined but is
an evocation of a figure beyond particularization. This hero is the essence
of humanity thinking, feeling, speaking. He is naked because he is free
from the confinement of form, like the snake of "Farewell to Florida"
who "left his skin upon the floor." This poem seeks a balance between
rage for order and desire to avoid order as a falsification. The goal is a
variation on Stevens's desire to make change itself a permanence.
Everything leads the observer toward the source of self, being itself:

> Item: The wind is never rounding O
> And, imageless, it is itself the most,
>
> Mouthing its constant smatter throughout space. (*CP*, 263)

This passage evokes the articulations of chaos as chaos creates forms.
Here the emphasis is not on experience, as in "Sunday Morning," but on
speech. Being becomes a stream in which things speak themselves, in
which the voice of the sea becomes one with the voice of the imagination
that remains a separate utterance in the earlier poem "The Idea of Order
at Key West."

The conclusion is another example of Stevens's self-destructing scaf-
folding: this perception too is an order, Stevens says, and no order can
endure. Devotion cannot be ritualized.

> And yet what good were yesterday's devotions?
> I affirm and then at midnight the great cat
> Leaps quickly from the fireside and is gone. (*CP*, 264)

Always the perceptions must be cast off, new ones to follow them. The
casting off is a part of the creative cycle. Yet in this case the image has its
own life and eludes the perceiver. The "great cat" is not a mere shell to
be sloughed off, like the snake's skin in other poems.

The notion that things speak themselves, that there is in fact a
"genius of the sea" with its own proper language, appears in two of the
most attractive and experimental poems in this collection, "Thunder by
the Musician" and "The Search for Sound Free from Motion." "The
Search for Sound Free from Motion" is a demonstration of "The world as

word": the typhoon speaks through the gramaphone, distorting the vehicle of voice into wind:

> All afternoon the gramaphoon,
> All afternoon the gramaphoon,
> The world as word,
> Parl-parled the West-Indian hurricane.

The conclusion articulates the demonstrated premise:

> The world lives as you live,
> Speaks as you speak, a creature that
> Repeats its vital words. . . . (CP, 268)

The "gramaphoon" distorts nature's utterances into human speech, yet they have a life of their own, beyond translation. Human language and the language of nature have certain points of crossing.

This notion of the crossing of human with inhuman speech also appears in "Thunder by the Musician," which posits a new kind of Thunderer, a musician who shows most clearly that "the gods come out of the weather," as Stevens says elsewhere. The thunder "became men"—"Mobs of ten thousand, clashing together, / This way and that." From this mob, a man emerged and "Held in his hand the suave egg-diamond / That had flashed" (CP, 220). The metaphor then becomes self-conscious, begins to self-criticize, self-destruct, to get back to the thunder itself as the voice of its own meaning. The thunder is at first inhabited, but then it inhabits itself and speaks its own language.

Stevens's concern with nobility and art, with poetry as a form of hero-ism, recurs throughout these poems. Trying still to deal with the war and with the claim that poetry has no place in such times, Stevens seeks to define the poet as the articulator of this martyrdom in such a way as to make the time able to read itself. In this way, the poet becomes a hero's hero. Yet these concerns are not the only focus of the collection, and Stevens's feelings about the value and function of art in wartime are, as always, ambivalent. During the composition of the poems, he wrote to the critic Hi Simons:

> Of course, what one is after in all these things is the discovery of a value that really suffices. Only last night I saw an expression in a French paper which is in point. It was something like this: "the primordial importance of spiritual values in time of war." The ordinary, everyday search of the

romantic mind is rewarded perhaps rather too lightly by the satisfaction that it finds in what is called reality. But if one happened to be playing checkers somewhere under the Maginot Line . . . one would spend a good deal of time thinking in order to make the situation seem reasonable, inevitable, and free from question. I suppose that, in the last analysis, my own main objective is to do that kind of thinking. On the other hand, the sort of poem that I have in the winter number of *The Kenyon Review* ["Variations on a Summer Day"], from which every bit of anything of that sort has been excluded, also has its justifications. (*LWS*, 346)

Never willing to limit his perspective, Stevens alternated his search for an appropriate voice for the war with a search for the pleasure of beauty, since, as his letter continued, "In a world permanently enigmatical, to see and hear agreeable things involves something more than mere imagism" (*LWS*, 346). One might argue that he himself alternated between the elegant woman seeker and the unnamed "figure of capable imagination" who defeats her in "Mrs. Alfred Uruguay." The word itself is exalted; the word is icon and salvation. The intelligence that informs it is not human, or not solely human.

"Of Modern Poetry," the most often anthologized poem of *Parts of a World*, makes a clear and direct statement of Stevens's definition of poetry at this time. It is demonstration as well as explanation of its thesis: Stevens creates a modern poem that is "Of Modern Poetry." The fragment that begins the poem is the basic definition that the rest of the poem enlarges and explains. Modern poetry is "the poem of the mind in the act of finding / What will suffice" (*CP*, 239). The fragment itself is a snapshot of action, continuous, undelimited. Poetry used to be conventions, like those of the theater; "the scene was set; it repeated what / was in the script." The poem is broken into three sections, the first break introducing, appropriately, the break with tradition. The forms and conventions are no longer appropriate in an age without traditional foundations: the theater "was changed," and its past "was a souvenir." The new poetry, to be a product of its time, must reflect the people and events of the contemporary world.

Suggesting by its very method how poetry might blur accepted boundaries and transcend the usual categories, "Of Modern Poetry" describes the new poetry as a medley of other arts and studies. Poetry is defined in terms of theater, music, philosophy. The contemporary audience will hear itself expressed through a poetry that is a blending by which the new world is made to fit or contain the new mind. The actor is

> A metaphysician in the dark, twanging
> An instrument, twanging a wiry string that gives
> Sounds passing through sudden rightnesses, wholly
> Containing the mind, below which it cannot descend,
> Beyond which it has no will to rise. (*CP*, 240)

"Sudden rightnesses" are the spiritual and aesthetic discoveries that the actor-poet must represent for his audience through his art. That the poet should simultaneously be actor, metaphysician, and musician is necessary to express in sound what the mind is. The next break introduces the possible subject matter of poetry, almost as an afterthought:

> It must
> Be the finding of a satisfaction, and may
> Be of a man skating, a woman dancing, a woman
> Combing. (*CP*, 240)

The particular action is not important. Action is the poem; the poem is the making of the poem, the poem becoming. "Of Modern Poetry" develops two of the three elements of artistic creation that Stevens defines in "Notes toward a Supreme Fiction"—"It must change" and "It must give pleasure"—and it must do so in an unpromising, unhappy world of war and disaster. To accomplish these tasks, the poet must be "a metaphysician in the dark." The books that followed gave shape and tone to his metaphysic.

Chapter Five

"He That of Repetition Is Most Master": *Transport to Summer*

Transport to Summer is Stevens's longest book and his most carefully arranged. It brings to harvest the ideas sown in *Parts of a World* and develops the concept of the "supreme fiction" as far as Stevens could take it as a substitute for religion. Stevens subsequently looks at the implications of his creation and reenvisions the supreme fiction as a religion itself. It is not yet Christianity, but it is like Christian mysticism, with a God and a concept of divine love that defines and manifests itself as continuing creation. Stevens's theism is now an Emersonian transcendentalism; it has yet to become human.

The five years between the publication of *Parts of a World* (1942) and the appearance of *Transport to Summer* (1947) were marked for Stevens by professional gains and personal losses. His last surviving sibling, Elizabeth Stevens MacFarland, succumbed to pneumonia during the unusually harsh winter of 1943, and his most devoted critic, Hi Simons, died suddenly of a heart attack in 1945. These years were not silent; Stevens published many poems and poem sequences. His work was sporadic and often interrupted, however, and his letters reflect his preoccupation with family matters and political events. Now that his generation was gone except for himself, he suddenly became involved with his siblings' children. Responding to a joint letter that some of his nieces and nephews had composed at a late-night gathering, he said, "I am a little hepped on family ties. It is one of the sources of strength in life."[1] His use of the singular "it" suggests that involvement with family ties was becoming a major presence in his life.

Although Stevens's association with the younger members of his family was a source of pleasure, it also brought him some problems. For instance, he championed the wartime wedding of his niece Jane MacFarland and gave the young couple a hefty gift as support, but when after a year the marriage failed, Stevens was so disappointed in Jane that he broke off what had been a warm and supportive correspondence with her. Only after many friendly overtures on Jane's part—she continued to write to him as though the relationship were uninterrupted—did he finally relent. His own daughter Holly also undertook a wartime marriage, much to her father's discomfort. Holly had first disappointed her father by dropping out of Vassar in the fall of 1942. She later explained that she had done so for two reasons: Vassar did not seem to be the real world ("I felt like a perfect ninny sitting by the Hudson River as an English major with a war going on"),[2] and she wanted to get a job so that she could establish her independence from an overly controlling family (Brazeau, 283). Stevens had pretended to go along with Holly's desire for independence; at the same time, he had attempted to arrange to pay someone at Vassar to pretend to be Holly's friend, keep an eye on her, and persuade her to stay there (*LWS*, 423–25). His stratagem failed: Holly quit school, got a job, and married an office machinery repairman. Her marriage to John Hanchak took place in the summer of 1944 and ended in divorce in 1951. Stevens's one grandchild, Peter Reed Hanchak, was born in 1947. It seemed that, in general, Stevens's relationships with real people (as opposed to his epistolary friendships with people he rarely or never met) were doomed to difficulty and often to failure. But they absorbed much of his creative energy during this time.

The critical reception of his last book may also have contributed to keeping him from issuing another full-length collection for a while. Reviews of *Parts of a World* were sparse and relatively unenthusiastic. "In not a single review of *Parts of a World* was there even so much as a suggestion that the book gave the man who read it any pleasure," he wrote his friend Henry Church (*LWS*, 430). Giving pleasure had always been one of Stevens's primary requirements for poetry, and his favorites among his poems were usually the ones he believed either provided pleasure in themselves or expressed well his axiom that poetry induces pleasure.

Stevens's reputation continued to grow on the basis of the earlier works, however, and his poetry was being translated into other languages. His presence as a major literary figure was underscored by his induction into the National Institute of Arts and Letters in 1946. Never fond of public speaking, Stevens nevertheless gave major addresses to large audiences at Mount Holyoke and Harvard. When *Transport to Summer* appeared at last in March 1947, it was reviewed enthusiastically. If pleasure was not referred to frequently in the reviews, significance and value were.[3] None of Stevens's previous books had received such immediate and widespread praise.

For many current scholars, this collection is the high point of Stevens's career and the true summer of his intellectual life. It contains what may be his most intensely studied and most often cited long poem, "Notes toward a Supreme Fiction," which is often referred to as the most explicit description of his poetic. It also contains "Esthétique du Mal"—another long poem that has intrigued and perplexed critics—as well as a number of frequently anthologized shorter works, "Of Modern Poetry" and "Man Carrying Thing," among them. *Transport to Summer* is a long, repetitious collection that defines the imagined land and the imaginative land in terms of heroism and conquest. It also goes further than Stevens had ever gone before in examining the moment of perception, in holding the mirror up to the poetic act. Here Stevens not only developed his meditative mode but refined the discursive form that characterizes his final period: three-line stanzas of flexible blank verse, reminiscent of Dante's tercets. *Transport to Summer* is a search that grows increasingly metaphysical in the act of finding, and it is appropriate that Dante should shadow the enterprise, as he did for the other major modernists Eliot and Pound.[4]

In *Transport to Summer*, Stevens explores and tests his description of poetry as "an act of the mind" (*CP*, 240), giving a comprehensive analysis and demonstration of the poetic act. A number of additional concerns punctuate this collection, which shows the poet, confronted by a threatening and unstable world, trying to find a way to let go of the past and hold on to it at the same time. Stevens's interest in genealogy and local history reached its high point during this period and is evidenced in his letters to his hired genealogists and in his poems. These poems also refine his argument justifying poetry. His attempts to define the poet-hero take second place as the focus passes from the figure of the maker to the act of making. Poetry, not only the poet, is granted selfhood. Poetry has a force beyond that of the individual creator; it is something like a Bergsonian life force. The soldier still appears, but the image is not foregrounded; the soldier-hero becomes one of many "major men" who are components or representatives of an abstract hero. (The soldier-hero still stands out occasionally, especially in the concluding section of "Notes toward a Supreme Fiction," but this poem was written during the war and before most of the rest of the poems.) In general, however, the presentation or description of the hero himself is not the primary objective any longer, although major figures of the apotheosis of the creator-poet surface and disappear throughout the poems. Stevens's hero is like the mythic "mesocosmic being," the "creature of a medial position" who, with his composite, larger-than-life figure, mediates between microcosm and macrocosm.[5]

From this point on, however, the focus is on the search for what Stevens called, in his letters to Sister Bernetta Quinn, the "centre" (*LWS*, 584) and on the directions and indirections of that search. The "centre" seems as much a matter of time as of place. Stevens in this period was much preoccupied with time: personal time, historical time, even the physics of time. As he wished his genealogical researchers to bring him the past, he attempts in his poetry to establish mythic linkages with the dead, to assimilate their essence and define himself through them. He is looking for what he describes in a poem title as "extraordinary references," even though he was pleased to define "the glass man" of "Montrachet-le-Jardin" as being "without external reference."

Coming to terms with the past, with the absolute division between past and present, is the theme of "Dutch Graves in Bucks County" and several other poems. "Dutch Graves" begins with the furor of the war-torn, vividly alive present, the past having vanished beyond memory: "And you, my semblables, in sooty residence / Tap skeleton drums inaudibly" (*CP*, 290). The Baudelairean refrain "mes semblables" that Stevens adapts is open and inclusive: the "semblables" are both the dead—Stevens's relatives—and, like Baudelaire's semblables, the readers, who are looking at the page from the distance of the future and sharing the mortality of speaker and ancestors as well as the poet's sharp awareness of transience.[6]

The present is described as a chaotic violence, "shouts and voices . . . / men shuffling on foot in air." As for the past, it is less than a memory: "the old flag of Holland / Flutters in tiny darkness" (*CP*, 290). Abruptly, the poem shifts from the emotion-filled present to the dead past in such a way as to evoke wonder at how completely the past has disappeared and at how that which was fully alive can just as fully vanish. The dead are totally gone, and yet they persist in a kind of ghostly continuity, present people and events resting on the unseen foundation of the past.

> What is this crackling of voices in the mind,
> This pitter-patter of archaic freedom,
> Of the thousands of freedoms except our own? (*CP*, 292)

The contrast between past and present sharpens, until the poem reaches its climactic assertion: "the stars, my semblables, chimeres, [*sic*] / Shine on the very living of those alive." Life is a force, a wave that passes across time. The "violent marchers of the present . . . March toward a generation's centre." The poem brings to mind Stevens's translation of Jean Le Roy's "Moment of Light," which appeared in *The Modern School* as far back as 1918. The Le Roy poem, which clearly stayed with Stevens, describes the lining up of the generations, with only one member spotlighted at a time.

> Before me, I know more,
> one smaller at the first, and then one smaller still,
> and more and more, that are my son and then his sons.
>
> They lie buried in dumb sleep,
> or bury themselves in the future. (*OP*, 142)

"Moment of Light" calls for those who are alive to make noises that will be memorials of themselves and signals to the future:

> Let us make signals in the air and cry aloud.
> We must leave a wide noise tolling
> In the night. . . . (*OP*, 143)

"Dutch Graves" looks back at the past more intensely than at the future as it explores the same mysteries as the Le Roy poem. The conclusion returns to the dead Dutchmen to dismiss them affectionately: "Time was not wasted in your subtle temples, / No: nor divergence made too steep to follow down" (*CP*, 293). This is a problematic conclusion (Are "temples" anatomic or architectural? Is it possible that they might be both?), but it may suggest that, though the past is no longer "living," it is not meaningless; nor are the dead so completely divorced from the present that their individual lives do not persistently affect those living today. The poem seeks a communication between past and present and finds it in a fiction that suggests the genetic presence of the dead ancestors in the representative of the present. Its alternating focus on the dead and on the present, "the very living of those alive," has the effect of affirming contradictory theses: that the past is erased and we must accept the clamor of the present as the only reality, and that the past continues to exert its subtle influence. We are asked to accept these two mutually exclusive propositions in an intuitively felt, logic-defying conclusion.

This kind of preoccupation recurs in "Extraordinary References," which describes a mother tying her daughter's hair ribbons and telling her the family history: "My Jacomyntje! Your great-grandfather was an

Indian fighter." The life stories, life cycles, of the ancestors constitute the "extraordinary references / Of ordinary people." They help constitute the sense of self of those presently alive by providing "references" that locate them in time. Thus, time too becomes a part of the mysterious web of personal identity, together with the (more ordinary) filaments of place. This kind of continuity helps assuage the sorrow of the young mother for her husband killed in the war by making of him a permanent link in the chain of generations. The conclusion of the poem may be seen as an attempt to undermine the myth:

> In the inherited garden, a second-hand
> Vertumnus creates an equilibrium.
> The child's three ribbons are in her plaited hair. (*CP*, 369)

The Romans associated the obscure Etruscan god Vertumnus with change, and he also appears at the center of the poisonous garden of Hawthorne's "Rappacini's Daughter." That this is a secondhand statue does not increase confidence in it, but the "second-hand Vertumnus" in "the inherited garden" may represent the fiction of familial continuity over the passing generations—a well-used bit of consolation, but better than nothing. The final image is of the girl, avatar of presence, hair tied with the ribbons of her heritage. For the mother, and presumably for the daughter too, there is a pleasure, an appropriateness, in this definition of self by lineage.

Transport to Summer is a long and multifaceted collection that represents a more philosophically oriented Stevens. Its earlier poems seem like a continuation of *Parts of a World*, while the last poems are more abstract and meditative, clearly drawing support from Stevens's readings in philosophy and aesthetics. (This placement cannot be seen as representing the development of Stevens's thought, as the poems are not arranged in the order composed. But he did choose to position them in this way, perhaps to showcase "Notes toward a Supreme Fiction" as a commentary on his other work.) Some of the concerns of *Transport to Summer* are further developments of *Harmonium* themes, although the treatment is more abstract and discursive. These poems take the relationship between mind and world far beyond the "Sunday Morning" conclusions. Place disappears as specific location to resurface as a concept. The real focus is time, although the time-place combination Stevens identifies as "weather" is also a constant. The desire for transcendence no longer meets a blank wall but instead finds intimations of divinity in nature abstracted and re-presented.

"The Pure Good of Theory" is a four-part meditation in Stevens's flexible tercets. It begins with the problem of time and finitude: "The mind that knows it is destroyed by time." We feel time passing as "a horse that runs in the heart" (*CP*, 329), a line that brings back Marlowe's Dr. Faustus, who, dying and damned, calls out for the horses of the night to slow down: "O lente, lente, currite noctis equi."[7] Against this awareness of limitation, we are invited to imagine "a large-sculptured, Platonic person" who is free from time. In part 2, this imagined person is pictured as an "emaciated / Romantic" who is unable to enjoy the holiday hotel, where the norm is a sensuous immersion in the present, because he is tortured by the question of what the senses mean and are. "Could the future rest on a sense and be beyond / Intelligence?" (*CP*, 331). The "Platonic person" finally discovers "a soul in the world"; that is, he discovers the animate other, which he then studies. This is one solution, or dissolution, to the mind-body problem: body may be subsumed in mind. Flesh may be a form of spirit after all. The degree to which Stevens is committing to the position is, of course, arguable—an "emaciated Romantic" cannot easily be seen as a heroic or even an admirable figure. Yet the possibility of this kind of monism is entertained as a hypothesis.

Part 3, "Fire-monsters in the Milky Brain," takes up from another perspective the question of the alienation of the human from nature. Adam was originally in a real world but created a false one through his perception. He fell into metaphor; metaphor is malformation. "He woke in a metaphor: this was / A metamorphosis of paradise" (*CP*, 331). Metaphor is a malformation created by need, by the desire for what is not. Part 4 explores further the meaning of metaphor. Reality or weather, the particulars of place are the source of our understanding. Our interpretations of the world are temporary and contain the seeds of their own destruction, but reality itself is limitless. Our need to touch it, to re-create it and thereby ourselves, is occasionally and gratifyingly met. "The Pure Good of Theory" exults in the changing weather, while it exalts meditation itself and posits a suggested meeting between mind and cosmos in which, temporarily at least, what is offered is what is most desired.

Another version of what in Stevens can be thought of as the mind-world problem is the short poem "Somnambulisma," structured as a simple argument. The poem describes two worlds, the world with imagination and the world without it. The "somnambulisma" of the title is the world without imagination, a dream motion or sleep life. Life would be merely a dream, the poem contends, if the world were not inhabited and mediated by the mind. But it is, and therefore life is not a dream.

The two parts of the major metaphor, bird and ocean, interact to demonstrate the poem's argument. The ocean is unstructured experience, reality. But the mind perceives the ocean as being like a bird; the bird is the imagination's product. The bird so resembles the water that one can hardly be distinguished from the other—a situation reminiscent of the relationship between the woman's song and the sound of the sea in "The Idea of Order at Key West." The bird is not permanent like the ocean; its generations are all "by water washed away" (*CP*, 304). The bird's existence, however, makes the difference between life as a sleep and life as vivid awareness. The bird is created by the "scholar." It is this imaginer who, by creating the bird from the ocean, gives others a structure or form by which they can grasp reality and waken to it.

Without interpretation, life would be meaningless, formless, a dream, the poem claims, but the interpretations must change and succeed each other. The highest good is the imagination creating, not the bird (poem) or sea (reality) but the scholar (mind). The poem's structure reinforces its meaning: the first nine lines describe the world with imagination, and the second the world without it. The first half shows the images of reality becoming part of the reality they reflect, and then passing away. The second half shows the world in which the raw material of the real remains unformed. Effectively, the "scholar" is not introduced until the end, when he is presented in a negative hypothesis: if he did not exist, then the world would be a dream. The figure of the scholar "separately dwelling" may be taken either as human imagination alone or as an early representation of the "external master of knowledge" who appears in Stevens's last poems. Either way, Stevens's concept of the imagination is becoming less clearly human and more exalted; it is developing a capital *I*.

Another poem about imaginative perception, "The Red Fern," has an imagist beginning. The red fern is the sun, in a metaphor similar to H.D.'s sea-pines. But the striking initial image is not the focus of the poem. The

> large-leaved day . . . opens in this familiar spot
> its unfamiliar, difficult fern,
> Pushing and pushing red after red. (*CP*, 365)

Sunrise and sunset seem fused in this opening picture. But the poem is about imaging, not about the image. The "red after red" is the energy in reality, which extends through space and is reflected off the air: "There are doubles of this fern in clouds." The echoes of the fern, "dangling seconds," are grown "beyond relation to the parent trunk," which is "the dazzling, bulging, brightest core" (*CP*, 365).

Thus does the sun create echoes of itself. Reality causes metaphor, this image suggests through the proliferation of the fern. Reality's echoes in the mind are its offshoots in the process of growth. Cognition or recognition follows. The poem follows Stevens's lifelong pattern of working through layers of possibility to an assertion, then retreating from the position, lowering the emotional intensity with a digression. Here the confrontation with the reality source is dropped with an ellipsis, and the poet turns to analysis instead of direct experience—the difference between "what you see" and real "sight" that "wakens the sleepy eye." What you see is inside, subjective: an infant's view. "Sight" is external. It invades, "wakens the sleepy eye." Thus, not only does reality cause metaphor, but reality intends metaphor as part of itself. This awakening suggests the "soul in the world" discovered by the "Platonic person" in "The Pure Good of Theory." The poem suggests another perspective that might be reached by the perceiver through his passionate attention to the real and lends more credibility to the positive assessment of the hypotheses of "The Pure Good of Theory."

The heroic poet-figure who surpasses "Mrs. Alfred Uruguay" in *Parts of a World* reappears transformed into a more abstract being in "Chocorua to Its Neighbor." The heroic figure here is presented in alchemical imagery; once more, Stevens inserts the reversible equation that alchemy is poetry. The poem begins with the difference between the particular and the abstract and describes the tendency of a particular to lend itself to abstraction:

> . . . a war
> Between cities is a gesticulation of forms,
> A swarming of number over number, not
> One foot approaching, one uplifted arm. (*CP*, 296)

The hero is then introduced as a person who comes out of the mountain's weather; he is an almost-realized form. He is a quintessence in which the four elements are mingled,

> a shell of dark blue glass, or ice,
> Or air collected in a deep assay,
> Or light embodied, or almost. . . . (*CP*, 297)

He is earth, water, air, and fire mixed in an assay, alchemy's traditional vessel. His presence gives meaning to the particulars, "enlarging," as he explains,

> the simplest soldier's cry
> In what I am, as he falls. Of what I am,
> The cry is part. (*CP*, 297)

Thus, the abstraction and the particular are interdependent in a mutual exchange of meaning. Like Rilke's unicorn who appears in the mirror because the young girl wants him, the hero exists "because men wanted him to be" but is nevertheless "physical if the eye is quick enough." Desire creates appearance.

The shadow that almost exists is mind speaking for itself, searching for itself, looking for its image in the glass as proof of its existence. This theme becomes dominant in other poems and is elaborated in "Notes toward a Supreme Fiction." The exact nature of the hero's voice will also be more fully explored in later poems, although the issue is addressed here:

> To say more than human things with human voice,
> That cannot be; to say human things with more
> Than human voice, that, also, cannot be;
> To speak humanly from the height or from the depth
> Of human things, that is acutest speech. (*CP*, 300)

The mountain is place, and the hero is mind. Mind emerges from place but is yet "human." The poem is the human being's search for self and place, nativity: rebirth as a native. The poem is elegiac rather than optimistic because its contradictions cannot be reconciled. Its true fulfillment would be the full and tangible incarnation of the hero, "of human realizings, rugged roy" (*CP*, 302). But to bring the hero into existence would freeze and therefore destroy him. Stevens grapples frequently with the problem that imagination must be human and yet cannot be merely human. "The chief defect of humanism is that it concerns human beings," he wrote to Henry Church in 1943. "Between humanism and something else, it might be possible to create an acceptable fiction" (*LWS*, 449).

The two major long poems of *Transport to Summer*, "Esthétique du Mal" and "Notes toward a Supreme Fiction," share many thematic similarities, although they are very different in style and tone. One would think "Esthétique du Mal" had been written first because it is more labored and uneven, but it was the later poem. In its attempt to account for evil in a world in which poetry keeps its stature as a good, it is like parts of *Owl's Clover*; it uses a similar verse form and, also like *Owl's Clover*, contains a plethora of topical references.[8]

The title telescopes Baudelaire's poetry of anguish, *Les Fleurs du mal* (1868), and his prose essays defining the philosophy and aesthetic for such poetry, *Curiosités esthétiques*.[9] The title sets up a rarefied and precious tone that is partly belied by the poem. For Baudelaire, poetry reflects the paradoxical relationship between beauty and horror, but it is a cover-up. Poetry is remote from reality, if not extraterrestrial; it is necessary, like clothing and makeup, to conceal the horror of naked humanity. In Baudelaire's work, naked reality is unbearable, whereas for Stevens it is the sought and cherished goal.[10] Stevens's lines "Be near me, touch my hand, phrases / Compounded of near relation" (*CP*, 317) locate poetry for him at the heart of the real and disclose it as a revelation of the essentially human.

Stevens commented that by *esthétique* he meant *aperçus*, indicating that he intended a series of insights into the nature of *mal* rather than a single conclusion (*LWS*, 469). But the poem is about aesthetics as well as it searches to accommodate evil in a human world that values beauty. Besides evil, *mal* means pain, and even difficulty or obstacle. The poem argues that in a kind of systolic and diastolic pulsation, we evade and confront the evils of life. Confrontation is heroic, but evasion is necessary. By finally refusing the various evasions the mind offers (discussed in the poem's series of parables), we approach the true center of reality, led there by the feelings, not by the mind, which is naturally evasive. At this theoretical center, the conceived and perceived worlds coincide; there is no need to strip or adorn reality (to confront or evade) because reality is poetry. (This junction is described more directly in "Notes toward a Supreme Fiction.")

Because the poem is not an essay but a series of "aperçus," there is no logical sequence of ideas, but instead a group of connected, related, and often repetitious statements. In part 1, the main persona of the poem, the investigator of "mal" is "at Naples, writing letters home" and "reading paragraphs / On the sublime" (*CP*, 313), an allusion no doubt to Longinus, whose *On the Sublime* describes the sublime as spirit or spark rather than technique. The direction the poem will take in its analysis, from the foreign and exotic to the homely and familiar, is set. Part 1 describes the split between the mind and the world that makes it

impossible for the mind to grasp pain. Pain is "human"—it is part of the
subjective—therefore it is essentially irrelevant both to the volcano and
to Longinus's philosophizing. The analyst of pain cannot get out of the
subjective to describe pain objectively. He is a prisoner within himself,
and neither his pain nor his comfort goes beyond himself. If animals are
discounted ("ignoring the cocks / that crow us up / To die"), then pain
is human only; it is no part of the world (*CP*, 314). Consciousness of pain
isolates the human being from the painless world.

Part 2 returns to the notion that pain does not exist outside of the
individual experiencing it. Projecting the anguish onto nature spoils
nature by falsification, making nature into a hallucination.

> Warblings became
> Too dark, too far, too much the accents of
> Afflicted sleep. . . .

Under these circumstances, the moon "evaded his mind" (*CP*, 314). The
moon's evasion may suggest the split of the poet's feeling self from his
thinking self. Concepts of pain are worthless. The "elegy" he "found in
space" is a resigned acceptance of this division and isolation. Pain is
"saved" by the fact that it is wholly human—that is, pain and pleasure
are known through the senses, not through the intellect, and therefore
they are part of the feeling self and real, rather than part of the thinking
self and hence a mental construction.

Part 3 rejects the traditional religious solution to the problem of evil,
perhaps represented by Dante. The passage appears to be a direct imita-
tion of Dante's terza rima, and Dante's *Divine Comedy* may well be the
"poem of heaven" that Stevens believed had "already been written."
"Fault" suggests both culpability and split. In an attempt to achieve
union with the divine, people created a god-man whose mythic superiority makes the actual isolation of the human situation more poignant and
unendurable. That is, the myth of union intensifies the reality of separation. This god can only "pity" man, from a divine level; sympathy can
come only from the same level. If this god were discredited and the reality of human pain considered on its own terms rather than in terms of
something else, human beings might come to be satisfied with their condition: "The honey of common summer / Might be enough" (*CP*, 316).

Parts 4 and 5 pick up the theme of pity versus sympathy. "Livre de
Toutes Sortes de Fleurs d'après Nature" brings Baudelaire to mind again,
but the connection may be misleading. These flowers may not be off-

shoots of Baudelaire's *Fleurs du mal*. Rather, the book title sounds much like a medieval herbal describing the flowers and their properties and uses. Such a book would be "sentimental" in assigning arbitrary meanings to the flowers without considering their true essences. The question is, Do we deal with evil by particularizing it and classifying it, as in the Christian solution and the allegorical universe? Do we assign a significance and a solution to each of its manifestations? Or do we accept it as part of a total in which everything is meaningful because the whole is an organism? Either way, what sort of art is engendered? In true romantic art (the "B." of the poem being possibly both Baudelaire and Brahms, the "dark familiar" from "Anglais mort à Florence"), does the committed artist, the "Spaniard of the rose," settle for a facile, imposed meaning instead of going after the truth of the thing as he perceives it, even though his vision may scarcely last long enough for its representation? The questions, of course, are loaded: the true artist seeks transparence, not opacity, and substitutes universal analogy for the analogical universe. He plays not "all sorts of notes" but one,

> In an ecstasy of its associates,
> Variations in the tones of a single sound,
> The last, or sounds so single they seemed one. . . . (*CP*, 316)

The "genius of misfortune," misfortune's daemon or presiding spirit, is the source of division—"fault / Falls out on everything" (*CP*, 316). Consciousness of evil causes us to further the fragmentation we are naturally heir to, wasting our creative energies in building up barriers against things that cannot be kept out or do not exist: "The genius of the body, which is our world, / Spent in the false engagements of the mind" (*CP*, 317). The "false engagements" contrast with the "true sympathizers" of part 5. Accepting pain means also accepting bliss. "In-bar" is human and "ex-bar," the objective or nonhuman in part 5, a climactic passage in which we are asked to heal the split within us by rejecting the falsifying intellect in favor of the feelings, which are genuine. This section is reminiscent of "Sunday Morning," but it is a more inward festival. Abstract knowledge is weighed against concrete experience. The greatest good, love, is not to be assigned to an external deity but to be fully experienced by human beings.

There is an abrupt change between the emotional, mind-centered part 5 and the remote intellectual parable of part 6, an enigmatic story about the sun and a bird. The sun seems to be nature, and the bird the mind; the fable is similar to that of "Somnambulisma." The bird and the sun are separate consciousnesses in a strange, unpeopled landscape. In the parable, change is the result of the world's desire for fulfillment. The world nourishes the mind, whose desires are like those of the world and yet irrevocably separate from them. The bird's hunger is flawed: he desires more than the world can give him. When his appetite is "corrected," when he learns, perhaps, to relish the world as it is, he still has "lapses" into hoping for and believing in a food other than the world, as well as "divinations of serene / Indulgence out of all celestial sight" (*CP*, 318). The bird, then, by his desire for the infinite, rejects the finite but satisfying experience of the sun, which is by the nature of things his.

Part 7 goes back to the human in its Whitmanian elegy for the soldier of time. It also looks at the human tendency to mythologize; the dead soldier and the woman become heroism and compassion, immortal because these qualities are immortal. The individual soldier exists in the idea of the soldier. The repetition of heroic sacrifice makes a ritual of it in which each individual act or enactment comes closer to articulating fully the meaning of the myth of self-sacrifice for the human good.

Part 8 speaks regretfully of the death of Satan. Satan is missed because with him go major fictions, "blue phenomena." Stevens is not merely lamenting the angels and circles of bright air of Dante's *Divine Comedy*; after all, in part 3 he called for an end to these. He may be lamenting the lack of a sense of cosmic evil deity and fatalism, like that which produced Baudelaire's malignant flowers, possibly another kind of "poem of hell," born of resignation to the appalling. Denial of possibility produces its own negative heroism—if not Baudelaire's Satanism, then Milton's Satan. But the poetry of negation and despair is not one in which the style is the natural outgrowth of the subject, any more than the structures of Pandemonium are natural to Milton's Hell. With the denial of the devil and the sense of fated evil comes the realization that the mind can penetrate the natural instead of trying to disguise it. The empty stage—even the deconstructed stage—is the scene for the new drama.

In part 9, the student of mal finds himself, like Crispin, divested of all the fictions he has lived by. The moon has deserted him. He is in a transitional stage, a period of decreation or divestment that will be followed by renewal. At the moment, he is a poet of "No," "prince of the proverbs of pure poverty" (*CP*, 320). The "indifferent crickets" may be the worn-out poets of the previous order, who will be drowned out by the "loud, large water," the force of nature whose primitive energy the new voice will sing. The poetry of No is not good poetry, Stevens argues, but this stage is necessary to the renewal that will come.

The "nostalgias" of part 10 are sentimental myths about nature and about the primeval union between natural and human. Reality is a beautiful woman, a mother-lover figure like the giantesses and sea-women who people Baudelaire's *Fleurs du mal*. To yield to nature, to be seduced by nature, would be "nostalgic," an attempt at an impossible union and thus ultimately another falsification. To yield to nature is to be absorbed by her and to deny the mind; nevertheless, it is necessary to approach reality and brave the danger. The student of mal struggles for rebirth and renewal instead of the peace offered by the "lovers of heaven and earth," those she-wolves and tigress-lovers who inhabit Baudelaire's poems, monster-women who represent the earth-mother devouring her son-lover.

Part 11 further explores the position that death is final, evil is within and without, and the church is dead. Only language is a positive value, as the frequently quoted lines explain: "Natives of poverty, children of malheur, / The gaiety of language is our seigneur" (*CP*, 322). Language is redemptive, and it is a force of gaiety in a world of misfortune. This insight is separated out from the rest of the section as a couplet. The student of mal has become the "man of bitter appetite" who will have nothing but truth and who reflects his mythless, barren weather. He is looking for a new mental framework in which his recently acquired knowledge makes sense.

Part 12 describes an attempt at restructuring. The seeker "disposes the world in categories," but this new order brings little relief. In neither the "peopled" (external and objective) nor the "unpeopled" (interior and subjective) world is there any escape from the isolation that consciousness brings. "In both, he is alone" (*CP*, 323). Therefore, he creates a third world, which is interior but does not contain reason. Here there is no judgment, only direct experience. Hence, "there is no pain," because nothing is judged good or ill, everything is only felt. The one trouble with this world is that it does not exist. The student is left with his original two unsatisfactory categories and the sense of loss that prompted the categorization. His attempt to deny pain by denying knowledge of pain has failed.

Part 13 alludes to the Genesis myth in its discussion of the origin of evil. How evil originated, as "punishment" or otherwise, is irrelevant. What is important is the fact of evil and what the perceiver makes of his fated isolation. The man in the cloister is the poet who has ceased to belabor his isolation and instead is inventing worlds. He has accepted the nature of reality and his coming death and is in a state of repose. He is a mythmaker, though perhaps not the ultimate mythmaker. There is too much of a yielding to reality in him, and his passivity is not in accord with Stevens's image of the poet as hero.

If the mythmaker of part 13 is too inclined to yield to reality, the revolutionary thinker in part 14 is much too resistant to it. Part 13 describes the domination of reason and the violence it engenders by trying to impose its structures on reality. Konstantinov can see only the structure of his delusion, which falsifies life. Looking too intensely at a part of reality leads to misapprehension of the whole. There are a multiplicity of worlds, each one the perspective of a single thinker, but the "logical lunatic" takes his view as the only one and tries to enforce his eccentric world as universal law. A lake, with its finite and describable limits, is logic, but the ocean defies logic. Reason banishes feeling, and feeling is contact with the actual: therefore, reason diverges from the actual. The dismissal of reason paves the way for the poem's final affirmation, which is of feeling.

It is the greatest poverty, according to part 15, to live according to the reason rather than the feelings; even if our rational constructions were true, they would be less desirable than what actually is. We are too limited to experience reality. The real lies always just beyond us, and should we penetrate it, we would find that it contains the metaphysical.

> . . . out of what one sees and out
> Of what one feels, who could have thought to make
> So many selves, so many sensuous worlds,
> As if the air, the mid-day air, was swarming
> With the metaphysical changes that occur,
> Merely in living as and where we live. (*CP*, 326)

These final lines take up Stevens's preoccupation with the relationship between the infinite number of perceptions and underlying reality. It appears that the imaginative visions were endemic in the air, in the world, and not merely in the eyes and ears of the beholder. Feelings, passions, senses, are more real than thought and lead to an intuited reality. A passage from the essay "Two or Three Ideas" is relevant to the poem's conclusion: "There is inherent in the words *the revelation of reality* a suggestion that there is a reality of or within or beneath the surface of reality. There are many realities through which poets pass constantly to and fro, without noticing the imaginary lines that divide one from the other" (*OP*, 265). These are the "metaphysical changes" of "Esthétique du Mal." They are as inherent in the real as they are products of the mind. Reality's gift is different from what was expected. What was sought after has come as a free gift, and at the center where the mind's world and the world coincide, the voice of the real is the human language.

The conclusion to "Esthétique du Mal" presents a fortunate discovery similar to that of "Notes toward a Supreme Fiction," but the latter poem is more abstract and less apologetic. "Notes toward a Supreme Fiction" is an ambitious and complex elaboration of Stevens's lifelong attempt to give art the position of religion. Its interpretation has been a major focus of Stevens criticism since the early 1980s. In discussing the poem, Stevens said, "In principle there appear to be certain characteristics of a supreme fiction *and the NOTES is confined to a statement of a few of those characteristics* [Stevens's emphasis]. As I see the subject, it could occupy a school of rabbis for the next few generations. In trying to create something as valid as the idea of God has been, and for that matter remains, the first necessity seems to be breadth" (*LWS*, 435). Stevens's ambivalence about the importance of God to the general scheme of things, seen in earlier letters, is present here in the parenthetical "and for that matter remains." The poem will show the blurring between poetry as the substitute for religion and as its equivalent. "Notes" was first published privately by Cummington Press, then included without change in *Transport to Summer*.

Excluded because of its length from most anthologies, this poem was not frequently singled out for special attention until the 1980s. Once it became the focus of critical interest, it compelled the attention of theoretically and philosophically oriented critics because of the cohesiveness of its argument and its congruency with contemporary attitudes toward historicity. Its structure is formal, consisting of three segments of ten sets of seven tercets each, followed by a final decade of tercets. Its triadic structure and its use of the tercet once more invites association with Dante's *Divine Comedy*, which Stevens not only invokes but echoes in this poem.

The dedication, "To Henry Church," was a last-minute addition; its position directly before the opening line ("And for what, except for you, do I feel love?") may mislead the unwary reader. The "you" addressed in the first line is not Henry Church but the fiction: the fiction is goddess and muse, self and other, and the language of the invocation's closing looks forward to "Final Soliloquy of the Interior Paramour."[11] The open-

ing of "Notes" concludes: "For a moment in the central of our being, /
The vivid transparence that you bring is peace" (*CP*, 380). The fiction is
comfort and companion, providing the solace of religion. It is the "centre" that Stevens has described as his goal, and the peace brought is presented as an epiphanic perception: a "vivid transparence" suggesting a
heightened clarity or true vision as well as vitality.

The first characteristic, abstraction, is defined in a Socratic address to
an "ephebe," or pupil, who is instructed to dump the truck of centuries
to see "the sun again with an ignorant eye / And see it clearly in the
idea of it" (*CP*, 380). The "ephebe" is instructed to rule out a creator for
the sun and to see it as itself, not in terms of something else. This is
nothing new—it is the stripping function that Stevens has always
required for rigorous poetic perception. The sun, the source, must "bear
no name, gold flourisher, but be / In the difficulty of what it is to be"
(*CP*, 381). The difficulty is plain, as the poem gives the sun a name even
in explaining why it must not be given one.

This first third of the poem explores the meaning of "the first idea";
to get at this meaning is to abstract. We are sent back to the first idea
by "the celestial ennui of apartments"—the careworn artificial constructions of our everyday fictions perhaps. The cycle of desire and disappointment is the motive for the return to the first idea, which,
however, is evasive, "the hermit in a poet's metaphors." Desire "knows
that what it has is what is not / And throws it away like a thing of
another time" (*CP*, 382). The human spirit is constantly in need of
refreshment. The poem is a means of sharing in the first idea "for a
moment," not permanently, because the instant something is articulated, it ceases to change and thus to live.

Poetry, then, revitalizes perception and serves as a medium between
subjective and objective. The section shifts from sun to moon in
describing the workings of the imagination: the "Arabian in my room"
is the moon, according to Stevens (*LWS*, 433), and moonwork is as
exhilarating as the sun's appearance. The fourth segment of "It Must Be
Abstract" analyzes the source of the first idea: not only our first consciousness of separation—Adam and Eve becoming self-aware in the
garden—but also, before human existence, the world's myth of itself. In
the "muddy centre" before human evolution, there was still "a myth
before the myth began" (*CP*, 383). Humankind became aware that the
world's myth was not the human story, and thus we began to sing our
own song:

> From this the poem springs: that we live in a place
> That is not our own, and, much more, not ourselves,
> And hard it is in spite of blazoned days. (*CP*, 386)

Our poetry mimicks the poetry of earth. The earth becomes a mirror for us, echoing us as we mimic it.

The following sections present the possibilities and difficulties of true "abstraction." Animals are introduced as elements and symbols of their places: the desert lion, the elephant of Ceylon, and the bear of the mountain are there for the ephebe to tame, but he is too timid to do anything but look out from the protection of his apartment and be overwhelmed by reality. The poem asks, How do imagined and real balance against one another in a true relation of mind and world? Does one issue boldly forth in search of the real? Does reality come to one, in sleep or awake? How can one court the interior paramour?

The epiphanies are quite possibly fortuitous: "Not balances / That we achieve but balances that happen." These are "moments of awakening," times when our intense personal experience of reality is far more real and direct than anything we could be taught: we "behold / The academies like structures in a mist" (*CP*, 386). Having then implied or presented something of the process of abstraction, the speaker turns to the poet himself. Who or what is the thinker of the first idea? As the first idea is an "imagined thing," it presupposes a "pensive giant" as imaginer. The problem is reconciling this "pensive giant" with MacCullough, the man who exists. The rest of the first part equates the major abstraction with "the idea of man." The speaker seems to be attempting to squint through the obscurity to glimpse "the inanimate, difficult visage." What surfaces finally is an old clown, a Charlie Chaplin figure who has been resurrected in part from "The Comedian as the Letter C," but who also has put in an appearance in "The Man with the Blue Guitar." This figure will be source and subject. "It is of him, ephebe, to make, to confect / The final elegance" (*CP*, 389). Abstraction for Stevens is the stripping of perception of those elements that localize it; it is a form of essentialism. This figure of power disguised as clownishness concludes the first segment of the poem.

"It Must Change" is almost a separate poem; the characteristics are individually defined and illustrated. The section begins with the image of sexuality and fruition—girls and bees, who pass before an "old seraph," one of Stevens's world-weary, sexually played-out observers, like the speaker of "Monocle de mon oncle." His jaded tastes find the change of seasons and beauties insufficient to tease his palate. A more fundamental, more complete change is required. The second tercet series begins, "The President ordains the bee to be / Immortal" (*CP*, 390), and suggests the impotence of the President in ordaining immortality. Anyway, his goal is misconceived. The bee is not supposed to be immortal, but the life force it represents is intended to be embodied in one generation after another. This force generates the heat in the desire that engenders.

The next question is the old preoccupation: What is the relationship between art and life? Making General DuPuy into a statue, an artifact, does not immortalize him but rather underscores his mortality. Changing "his true flesh to an inhuman bronze" falsifies and demeans him. The bee and the statue remain opposites, life and art. Part 4 begins the series of matings and copulations that illustrate the dynamic of change.

> Two things of opposite natures seem to depend
> On one another, as a man depends
> On a woman, day on night, the imagined
>
> On the real. This is the origin of change.
> Winter and spring, cold copulars, embrace,
> And forth the particulars of rapture come. (*CP*, 392)

Poetry is no longer an "up and down between two elements," as it is for Crispin. It is a dialectical movement, one that is never resolved but immediately upon synthesis opposes a new pair of opposites. The matings result only in a brief sharing. The observer becomes the observed, growing and changing but then seeing from a new perspective, which changes the observation. It is a movement of friendly pursuit:

> The child that touches takes character from the thing,
> The body, it touches. The captain and his men
>
> Are one and the sailor and the sea are one.
> Follow after, O my companion, my fellow, my self,
> Sister and solace, brother and delight. (*CP*, 392)

The passage echoes Whitman, suggesting the expansive inclusiveness of both "Song of Myself" and "There Was a Child Went Forth." These climactic lines assert joy and empowerment through participation in reality.

As is so often the case, Stevens immediately retreats from the extreme position. Part 5 is an elegy for another kind of realist, a Crispin-like figure. The planter lived his life genuinely if not fully, and although his level of self-awareness was not high, nevertheless he was not "an unaffected man in a negative light." The tone shifts from exaltation to elegy. Part 6 returns to a consideration of the romantic, and to the cacophony of romantic birds that Stevens disposed of in "The Man on the Dump" and elsewhere. These peevish birds provide no solace, only the annoying garble of a false intimacy—a constant "bethouing," or *tutoyant*. Stevens, who was addressed by his first name by very few, was intrigued by other languages' familiar form of address, which he used to suggest a familiarity beyond barriers. The movement of the poem is back to bareness or spareness as preparation for another mystic marriage: we do not need paradise, argues part 7, in notes reminiscent of "Sunday Morning." The payoff for living in the world is living in the world. These comments lead into the parable in part 8, in which Shelley's Ozymandias is betrothed to Nanzia Nunzio. Ozymandias can be understood as mind, imagination; but perhaps he is also the poet who perceives his own completion, realizes that he will not outlast his life. He thus holds the opposite attitude from that of Shelley's Ozymandias. The woman speaks to him of her nakedness, and he points out that she can never be naked:

> The bride
> Is never naked. A fictive covering
> Weaves always glistening from the heart and mind. (*CP*, 396)

The world is never perceived directly, but always perception remains veiled by the subjectivity of the perceiver.

Given the uncertainties of both vision and language, what does the poet do? What is the poem? Part 9 notes that the poet is always in search of the speech that will be apposite to the conception. He tries to put the ineffable or inexpressible into the world's words: "To compound the imagination's Latin with / The lingua franca et jocundissima" (*CP*, 397). The last section leaves the reader with the thinker on a bench in the park, allowing the changing scenes to impinge upon his consciousness. Shelley is again a presence here, his west wind identified with "a will to change." This will is part of the basic human drive, perhaps what makes us human or what is most human in us.

"It Must Give Pleasure" begins by invoking, and then dismissing, images of Christianity as the route to delight. The "facile exercise" that

is the common worship is linked to Saint Jerome, who translated the
Bible. This kind of shared myth has its satisfactions but requires little of
the partaker. The common worship or group myth is contrasted with the
"difficultest rigor" of a relation with reality that is not prefabricated or
static but always under challenge. The moment of poetry is discovery;
the "reason" comes later. The moments of discovery are irrational, and
we are attempting to understand the irrational in creating poetry. The
echo of Hopkins ("heaven-haven") may suggest that Hopkins within the
Christian framework was practicing a perception-based poetic. Part 2
gives an image of a "blue woman" who may be a muse of change and of
the pleasure that change brings; this kind of change, the waxing and
waning of nature, is associated with sexuality. The next section brings in
God again and suggests a contrast between graven images of God: "A
face of stone in an unending red . . . An ancient forehead hung with
heavy hair" (*CP*, 400), and the unfixable idea of God that produces these
images. The genesis of godhead is described: "A dead shepherd brought
tremendous chords from hell / And bade the sheep carouse" (*CP*, 400).
The figure combines Orpheus with Christ, both mesomorphic figures, in
a melding of vatic and divine.

Another pair of divine spouses in part 4 provides a new interpretation
of the marriage of mind and world. This time the bride is "Bawda," the
bawdy, the chthonic. Her mate is "a great captain" who marries Bawda
because she loved the place she comes from and represents. She loves
him "as she loved the sun"—for his life force, with which he energizes
her. They "married well because the marriage-place / Was what they
loved" (*CP*, 401). It is weather that provides pleasure, weather being all
the sensory conditions and changes that the environment provides and
the physical manifestation of spirit.

"Canon Aspirin" and his sister next appear on the scene, another
male-female pair who are this time not lovers but complements. The
canon, according to Stevens, is "the sophisticated man" who has searched
for but not found a sufficing fiction (*LWS*, 445). The sister avoids the
search entirely, hiding from the risk and hiding her two children from it.
Hers is a "reality" of diminishment. The canon seems not to be thorough
enough in his intellectual rigors to complete his imaginative work.
Therefore, he ends up with an unsatisfying patchwork fiction. He
perhaps—as Stevens may have presumed an actual canon would do—
creates orders rather than discovers them, and this is a lesser accomplish-
ment: "to impose is not to discover." His name suggests that he is
looking for a cure for the cosmic headache, but he does not find one, per-

haps because his tentative solutions are too much like aspirin. Part 7 raises the question of whether it is possible to discover reality, to reach a point at which discovery is creation, to go beyond the facile solutions through total involvement so that one arrives at the center. The answer is that "It must / Be possible."

> The real will from its crude compoundings come,
>
> Seeming, at first, a beast disgorged, unlike,
> Warmed by a desperate milk. To find the real,
> To be stripped of every fiction except one,
>
> The fiction of an absolute—Angel,
> Be silent in your luminous cloud and hear
> The luminous melody of proper sound. (*CP*, 404)

Of course, Stevens at once interrogates this precipitous position. Helen Vendler, in her provocative analysis of the major allegorical personae in "Notes," suggests that the angle is merely another illusory figure to be dismissed, on Stevens's way to a more terrestrial fiction.[12] But the lyricism of the passage does not support dismissal of the angel; rather, it suggests that this fiction is "for the moment final," that it is to be withdrawn from in awe. Nor does Stevens evoke and dismiss his personae like morality-play vices; instead, he entertains their extreme positions and then flees from their implications. He is like the cartoon characters who walk out on a limb until they are standing on air but do not fall until they look down. Part 8 begins with the question, "What am I to believe?" The image in this section is of the angel, self-aware and forgetful of his heaven, taking pleasure only in the motion of his flight. Stevens identifies with this creation-become-creator; he asks, "Is it he or I that experience [*sic*] this?" This merging of creator, action, and created object produces "inexpressible bliss," which, though temporary, is completely fulfilling: "I have not but I am and as I am, I am" (*CP*, 405).

The inevitable retreat follows, but the moment of bliss casts its light on the whole process of creation and decreation that constitutes human endeavor. The "repetitions" of the robin (or the poet) are "an occupation, an exercise, a work, / A thing final in itself and therefore good" (*CP*, 405). He finds from the glimpse of the real and imaginary angel that "merely going round is a final good." The conclusion of this diminished assertion is that

> Perhaps,
> The man-hero is not the exceptional monster,
> But he that of repetition is most master. (*CP*, 406)

The next section is one of the most intensely discussed poems in Stevens. It is about the last of the series of male-female relationships that describe the mind-world problem, and its tone is ambiguous. The "fat girl" is the world, and this ultimate courtship is formal, genteel, culminating in naming rather than copulation. Naming is control, and the metaphor is sexual possession:

> . . . underneath
> A tree, this unprovoked sensation requires
> That I should name you flatly, waste no words,
> Check your evasions. (*CP*, 406)

What she is, what exists between them, is "The fiction that results from feeling" (*CP*, 406).

The supreme fiction is defined in this culminating section as perception beyond reason. Reason comes later: "They will get it straight one day at the Sorbonne." This melding of knowledge and intuition will allow him to name her and make her transparent, a text that he can fully read.

> Until flicked by feeling, in a gildered street,
> I call you my name, my green, my fluent mundo.
> You will have stopped revolving except in crystal. (*CP*, 407)

This moving fixity, this transparent green, is the point of oxymoronic resolutions, "world" and "mind" becoming one through the power of the word.

The thirty-first series of seven tercets is addressed to "Soldier" and attempts to show how poetry is not merely a private enterprise, a personal alchemy, but also gives life to real-world events and engagements. "The soldier is poor without the poet's lines." The envoi serves both as a link to the war concerns and as a diffusion of the intensity at the end of "It Must Give Pleasure."[13]

"Notes" was written early on in the period covered by *Transport to Summer*, but Stevens chose the poem to conclude the collection. It serves as the high point of his concern with the "supreme fiction" and as the most complete definition of it. Although he began thinking of the supreme fiction as poetry, he changed his mind as he proceeded. In a letter to the Cummington Press while still engaged in writing the poem, Stevens said, "These are three notes by way of defining the characteristics of supreme fiction. By supreme fiction, of course, I mean poetry" (*LWS*, 407). Later, Stevens indicated that the supreme fiction was not to be limited to poetry, and that it remained for him undefined. To Hi Simons, he wrote, "I think I said in my last letter to you that the Supreme Fiction is not poetry, but I also said that I don't know what it is going to be. Let us think about it and not say that our abstraction is this, that or the other" (*LWS*, 438). It may be that he was extending an invitation to the supreme fiction to define itself, through him. In any case, his late poems show an attempt to represent the supreme fiction as something beyond poetry, something to which poetry is an approach.

Chapter Six

"An Abstraction Blooded":
The Auroras of Autumn

Stevens's correspondence, like the correspondence of any other person of letters, is an index to his changing needs and desires. His early letters are mostly to Elsie, showing the extent of his identification of the romantic with her; the letters to friends and business associates, the requests for art and art objects that represented places for him, and the intense genealogical inquiries, all show his subsequent investments of the romantic in place and in historical connections. In the letters as well as the poems, he develops the complex concept of place that has always been central to his work. Place becomes a physical-metaphysical locus where change intersects timelessness. The lush Florida landscape has long given way to New Haven. It is, moreover, a New Haven of the mind, perhaps a New Heaven.

In his last period, two important correspondents mark the new direction of his quest. His letters to Sister Bernetta Quinn, O.S.F., and to the Irish poet Tom McGreevy show his greater attraction to a traditional spirituality than he had previously experienced; both of these epistolary friendships began in 1948. The letters suggest that Stevens found reflected in the Franciscan nun and the Catholic poet those elements of religion that brought him toward his final decision to join the Roman Catholic Church. Stevens frequently mentions McGreevy's Catholicism in the same breath as his Irishness, and more than once Stevens comments on the notion that for the Irish, God is one of the family. The idea of a familiar deity, a God who would *tutoyer* the poet or address him familiarly and would also be so addressed, appealed to the man who was on a first-name basis with very few and who referred to his wife as "Mrs. Stevens." In "Our Stars Come from Ireland," Stevens uses McGreevy's imagined thoughts of Ireland as the basis for an equivocal poem that suggests the promise of the Resurrection. The McGreevy-Stevens correspondence, largely overlooked by critics, is as extensive and detailed as Stevens's correspondence with José Rodriguez Feo, a body of letters that has been published as a book and analyzed in detail.[1] Comparing the two

sets of letters shows the McGreevy-Stevens correspondence to be more
low-key, less ferociously focused on poetry, and more personally revealing on Stevens's part. As Stevens identified his earthier, more physical
self with Feo and Feo's environment, he found imagery for his spiritual
leanings in McGreevy and the Irish poet's concept of home.

Sister Bernetta Quinn is more connected in Stevens's thought with
Christian scholarship, Christian literary analysis, and the iconography of
traditional religion. Through his correspondence with her, the symbols
were reempowered for Stevens. He initially evaded her Christian interpretations of his work, claiming not that they were incorrect but that
they limited him.[2] But he grew more and more appreciative of her analysis and her perspective. His first published letter to her, in April 1948,
included the comment, "I don't want to turn to stone under your very
eyes by saying 'This is the centre that I seek and this alone.' Your mind
is too much like my own for it to seem to be an evasion on my part to
say merely that I do seek a centre and expect to go on seeking it" (*LWS*,
584). Stevens came to associate Sister Bernetta with Easter, a celebration
that perhaps had more appeal to him than Christmas, which he tended
to find depressing. "I enjoyed your Easter greeting," he wrote to Sister
Bernetta in 1953. "Your notes bring me into contact with something I
should not have otherwise except for them and I am grateful to you"
(*LWS*, 774). The lack he refers to here might have been the Christian
symbolism reilluminated for him by her faith and scholarship.

Moreover, his myth of home and the family began to converge with
memories of his Christian childhood and recognition of the sadness of
transience. The "Sunday Morning" philosophy of joy in flux is nearly
inverted in one of his last letters to Sister Bernetta, this one in response
to a Christmas greeting:

> It does me more good than I can tell you to have your Holiday Greetings.
> These, somehow or other, take me back to a much simpler world of home
> which, while it is gone for good, is still a good deal more permanent than
> the present world can ever be. . . . Part of your letter is part of the season
> of the year and the season of the year is part of the world that has dis-
> appeared. (*LWS*, 807)

Stevens's last ten years were marked by international fame and the
highest national awards. His election to the National Institute of Arts
and Letters in 1945 was followed by two National Book Awards, the
prestigious Bollingen Prize, and a Pulitzer Prize in the year of his death.

His career as an insurance executive had also prospered, providing him with the financial security his father had taught him to value. The stresses of being a conservative in a liberal literary community were alleviated by a general drift to the right, demonstrated in the writers John Steinbeck, John Dos Passos, and others whose political shift was less obvious. The threats to Stevens's personal sense of security were diminished by the war's end and by the general feeling of optimism that persisted even in the midst of the postwar depression.

Stevens's personal life had reached an equilibrium. Elsie had moved to the periphery of his life, quite possibly to the relief of both. She occupied her suite at Westerly Terrace, spent much of her time gardening, and took care of the house with the aid of various hired women who often found her too exacting and did not stay long (Brazeau, 233–40). The Stevenses very rarely entertained, but those few guests they did invite for a meal commented on Elsie's fine cooking and personal reticence. It appeared to some that Stevens was embarrassed by his wife's lack of education and did not encourage her to take part in conversations. But Stevens's relationship with his daughter Holly improved, even as her marriage deteriorated. She had married at least partly out of rebellion; the increasingly frequent marital disagreements suggested to her that her father had been right. As she drew away from her husband, her father provided more and more support for her. When she finally was divorced in 1951 and given custody of her son Peter, her father gave her an apartment and a stipend so that she would not have to go back to work (Brazeau, 285). He also began taking her to literary events with him and introducing her to friends who had never even seen Elsie. Holly became a kind of informal literary secretary for him, keeping track of events and escorting him to them. (Neither he nor Elsie had ever learned to drive.) He had a high respect for Holly's business acumen and organizational capabilities and grew to rely on her. In the last couple of years of Stevens's life, when he had slowed visibly, she was nearly always with him at readings and on other public occasions. Stevens was pleased that he could support Holly and his grandson easily and maintain his own establishment as well. He also felt that in some important way Holly had come home.

But material security and family stability, once achieved, were no longer sufficient for him. His intellectual researches, never having diminished in intensity, now were finding new directions: he was reading mystical and religious materials, as well as the speculative philosophy that had always interested him. He was sustaining more correspondences and friendships with people of religious commitment. In his last years, religious books and pamphlets came to the office; his coworkers speculated about them. Moreover, he apparently satisfied his growing curiosity about the Roman Catholic faith by asking questions of his Catholic friends the Sigmans, who then discussed them with a priest, the Reverend Cassian Yuhaus.[3] Stevens's late poems reflect these metaphysical considerations as he looked toward the end of his life and his fictions. The poems of his last two collections focus on the meaning of being, the definition of perception, and the source and meaning of desire. They both elegize and celebrate the life of the mind from the perspective of late middle age, and they exalt imagination as a literally divine force. Their metaphysic is much more visible than it is in the earlier poems. The tenor and vehicle of his major metaphors converge. The sun is no longer a metaphor for creativity, but it becomes creativity itself. It is only a step for the cosmic images to be absorbed into the notion of a divine power source.

The last phase of Stevens's work begins with *The Auroras of Autumn* (1950). Stevens thought of his *Collected Poems* as an organic whole; he originally wanted to call it *The Whole of Harmonium* (*LWS*, 834). As he was finishing the *Autumn* poems, his editors had begun asking him for an edition of his life works, but he felt that it was not time yet. (Unlike many other poets, he seems to have thought of an edition of his collected poems as a finality [*LWS*, 829, and elsewhere].) Nevertheless, *The Auroras of Autumn* is dominated by the tone of valediction that characterizes much of his late work. His concerns shift from the scenes of fulfillment, the definition of the poet as hero, and the action that is poetry to consideration of the poem as product and the meaning of having-created. The elegiac tone heightens as the awareness of finitude becomes a prevailing note. As Stevens ages and approaches his last work, he runs a constant retrospective analysis of what it means to be, or to have been, a poet. The elegy for the individual self, however, yields to glimpses and intimations of a whole greater than the self and of a renewal beyond the power of human imagining. The cycle of his seasons continues beyond winter to beginnings of a new spring in the final section of *The Collected Poems*, "The Rock," and in other late poems. His last poems attempt to strip the final veil between the mind and the real, between self and other. "The elementary idea of God is a face: a lasting visage in a lasting bush," he wrote to Hi Simons in 1942 (*LWS*, 438). His late work attempts to look directly upon the face of God.

At the time of this concluding work, he also published a collection of his essays, *The Necessary Angel* (1951). Its title is taken from the last poem of *The Auroras of Autumn*, "Angel Surrounded by Paysans" (to be discussed later). The angel of reality, "the necessary angel of earth" (*CP*, 496), is he who dismantles the past to enable reconstruction. The dates of composition of these essays range from 1942 to 1951, and they represent the bulk of Stevens's nonepistolary prose. Unlike Pound and Eliot, Stevens did not go in much for prose commentary on poetry, and almost all the prose pieces he produced were written in response to specific requests for addresses and articles. These essays are useful as glosses on the longer poems written concurrently with them, although one might argue that the positions are represented much more clearly in the poems. In any case, the essays suggest, through the readings he quotes and cites throughout the book, which of these readings seem to have had the greatest effect on his poetics.

Specific preoccupations of Stevens's late work include the world as mind, a kind of transparence; the self-destruction of language as it fulfills itself; the existence of a Jungian collective unconscious that seems to manifest itself sometimes as a metaphor for psychic history and sometimes as a literal truth; and the effort to "read" this reality that, seen without the shadows of human interpretation, represents the mind of God. In 1948 he wrote to his friend Barbara Church, "Thinking about the nature of our relation to what one sees out of the window, for example, without any effort to see to the bottom of things, may some day disclose a force capable of destroying nihilism" (*LWS*, 602). In *The Auroras of Autumn*, Stevens conflates force and imagination to produce a dynamic concept of God.

These poems also provide various articulations of Stevens's most painful question: Is poetry real? Or, more immediately, Is *my* poetry real? It is these late poems that lend themselves most to phenomenological criticism, for their emphasis on being and on the nature of perception suggests both Husserl and Heidegger. Thomas Hines's insightful study *The Later Poems of Wallace Stevens* (1976) analyzes the later poems as descriptions of phenomenological concepts and practices and shows how Stevens's tropes, images, and structures provide solid support for this theory.[4] The definitions and demonstrations of the nature of perception in Stevens's late poems make it possible to read them as a demonstration of phenomenology in action, particularly of the more mystical, Husserlian version of phenomenology.

The Auroras of Autumn is a comparatively short collection for Stevens, and the poems vacillate between intense involvement and meditative retreat. The question of self is entangled with the question of God.

"Does my poetry get anywhere?" is inextricable from the question of whether there is anywhere for it to go. The title poem has an apocalyptic urgency. As the year of his poems draws toward its end, the intensity of the desire they express increases and their tendency to qualify their positions decreases. "Auroras" comes close to making a straightforward assertion. Written in his late discursive style of decades of tercets (here a single decade of eight-tercet units), the poem is both elegiac about the limits of an individual life and affirmative about the possibility of completing the life's task of finding/creating "what will suffice" (*CP*, 239).

The first segment of "Auroras" reintroduces the snake, one of Stevens's earlier figures of both change and power. In "Farewell to Florida," the snake "left its skin upon the floor" as the speaker sought new fictions. Here the snake is "bodiless," the undefined shade of itself, a decreated fiction with power to reconstitute itself. "His head is air"; its very existence is in doubt, and it may be an illusion or distortion—it may be merely "another image at the end of the cave" of Plato's parable. The snake, personalized and gendered by the pronoun *he*, has the characteristics of the supreme fiction—"he" is abstracted ("bodiless"), changing ("form gulping after formlessness"), and pleasure-related ("in possession of happiness"). Like the mountain hero of "Chocorua to Its Neighbor," the snake is only *almost* a presence, glimpsed by his movements, half-seen and half-imagined. Ironically, it is part of "his" snake nature that we do not fully believe in him, that we do not accept his self-creation.

> These lights may finally attain a pole
> In the midmost midnight and find the serpent there,
>
> In another nest, the master of the maze
> Of body and air and forms and images,
> Relentlessly in possession of happiness.
>
> This is his poison: that we should disbelieve
> Even that. His meditations in the ferns,
> When he moved so slightly to make sure of the sun,
>
> Made us no less as sure. We saw in his head,
> Black beaded on the rock, the flecked animal,
> The moving grass, the Indian in his glade. (*CP*, 411–12)

It could be argued that the "snake" and the "master of the maze" are two figures, but the section coheres better if they are seen as blurred and

melded, the imaginer imagining himself. The snake is very different
from all of Stevens's earlier figures of the imagination, such as the
woman singing in "The Idea of Order at Key West" and the young
horseman of "Mrs. Alfred Uruguay." The snake represents the imagination as sheer potency, undelimited and without content. The power is
almost impersonal but not quite, as it is still defined by the pronoun *he*.
The passage serves as an invocation to the god-muse, who then slips in
and out of the poem like a snake, now visible, now only suggested by a
movement.

The second three sections comprise an elegy for a fiction that is being
discarded, the fiction of the human parents and children, that old Hegel-
ian unit of thesis, antithesis, and synthesis that appears throughout
Stevens's work. Each of these sections begins "Farewell to an idea . . .,"
and the triple repetition has the effect of a ritualized farewell. This fiction is gone, dismissed and exorcised. The new fiction must go beyond
the human, and hence our dearest myths must pass away.

The awe of the individual in the face of death is represented by the
scene of a deserted cabin and a man who walks along the beach, watch-
ing the aurora borealis, which is described as bursts of color and light:

> . . . its blue-red sweeps
> And gusts of great enkindlings, its polar green,
> The color of ice and fire and solitude. (*CP*, 413)

Commentators have noted that the explosive, fiery images in this poem
are associated with the explosion of the atom bomb. This reading is persuasive, since "Auroras" was written shortly after the war, when pictures
of Hiroshima and Nagasaki were on the front pages of all the newspapers and in everyone's mind. But such an interpretation fails to explain
the positive elements in the poem, the cleansing and revitalizing power
of this overwhelming force. It may be that images of nuclear cataclysm
combine with nature images to produce an overall impression of the
total destruction of a world order, although this destruction may be of
natural causes and intended as part of the overall scheme of things. The
walking witness in the poem is dwarfed by the immense changes he perceives.

Part 3 shifts from the man walking outside to the figure of the
woman in the house, mother and muse: "The mother's face, / The purpose of the poem, fills the room" (*CP*, 413). She is old, fading, no longer
able to nourish; her purpose is fulfilled as mother and muse. The cata-

clysm is about to begin: "A wind will spread its windy grandeurs round / And knock like a rifle-butt against the door" (*CP*, 413). There will be an abrupt end to the order they have known. The house and the books will be destroyed, and "Boreal night / Will look like frost as it approaches them" (*CP*, 413). Frost is one of Stevens's early and frequent symbols of death. But what approaches is not frost, although this is how it appears. It is the coldest of northern nights, with the flashing luminosity of the aurora borealis, a darkness shot through with an alien and unpredictable illumination. It is ordinary time confronted with eternity, finitude with infinity.

Part 4 indicates that the end is not the end, "The cancellings, / The negations are never final" (*CP*, 414). The cosmic comedy will recommence. The section concludes with what may be taken as an invocation to the power of mind, perhaps another figure of the snake-master of the maze that begins the poem:

> Master O master seated by the fire
> And yet in space and motionless and yet
> Of motion the ever-brightening origin,
>
> Profound, and yet the king and yet the crown,
> Look at this present throne. What company,
> In masks, can choir it with the naked wind? (*CP*, 414–15)

The question suggests the difficulty of finite mind producing anything that has a true accord with reality, since reality is infinite and forever changing. No voice can speak with the wind's voice. The passage recalls the mingling of the singer's voice with the sea sounds in "The Idea of Order at Key West." Here reality is not translatable into song, for the disproportion between the individual consciousness and the vastness of being is too great. It is useful to contrast the relationship between speaker and nature in "The Idea of Order" and "Auroras." In the earlier poem, speaker, imagination, and reality are clearly defined, and their independence remains unchanging despite the intercourse between them. In "Auroras," there is an overwhelming and frightening invasion of self by other. This invasion is destruction and purification at once, similar to the experiences of the great mystics, such as Saint John of the Cross (whose work Stevens had read).

Part 5 centers again on the family as muse, director, and audience of the human story, but the family's theater or festival falls far short of the

ideal, and its play does not ring true. Part 6 describes a contrasting theater, which may be seen as the theater of reality. This is an overwhelming spectacle of change and light.

> It is of cloud transformed
> To cloud transformed again, idly, the way
> A season changes color to no end,
>
> Except the lavishing of itself in change. . . . (CP, 416)

As "the cloud drifts idly through half thought-of forms," the reader may
think once more of the mushroom-shaped cloud so recently in the public
mind when the poem was written. But the conclusion of the segment,
though its images might seem an appropriate presentation of a bomb
blast, is not appropriate emotionally:

> He opens the door of his house
>
> On flames. The scholar of one candle sees
> An Arctic effulgence flaring on the frame
> Of everything he is. And he feels afraid. (CP, 416–17)

"Feeling afraid" would be a weak phrase to describe one faced with
nuclear holocaust, but it is appropriate for the awe that the scholar
whose light is single and flickering might feel when confronted by imagination, mind in the abstract. At the end of the cycle of change, the seasons of the year, comes the cold northern light of the aurora borealis.
This purest light, this "Arctic effulgence" of the fable, is easily equated
with the source-imagination, the possibility of which is then described
again in part 7.

> Is there an imagination that sits enthroned
> As grim as it is benevolent, the just
> And the unjust, which in the midst of summer stops
>
> To imagine winter? (CP, 417)

The imagination is first introduced as a hypothesis, in the form of a
question, but question changes to statement as the section proceeds: "It
leaps through us, through all our heavens leaps." The imagination
briefly illuminates all through which it passes, as the aurora borealis illu-

mines the northern skies. Moreover, it "dare not leap by chance in its own dark." The imagination, the world-spirit, is directed by "slight caprice" (*CP*, 417). There is a will to things. At this point, this external will seems more like a form of abstract theism than like the Christian God, but it is present as a potent, however amorphous, force.

Part 8 takes up the notion of innocence, a problematic concept that Stevens had explored in "Esthétique du Mal." If some sort of spirit of "genius" is ascribed to the earth, is it innocent or malign? The aurora borealis marks a conclusion, or death. Is the existence of death the sign of an unfriendly cosmos? No, says the poem, death is part of a whole that is innocent, as we are innocent. Our sense of alienation does not come from our guilt. Part 9 retreats again to our awareness of this alien-ation and looks back on a golden age when we were able at least to believe that we were at one with our surroundings: "We were as Danes in Denmark," believing that we were "brothers," taking pleasure in the senses, "fed / And fattened as on a decorous honeycomb" (*CP*, 419). The illusory notion of belonging has been destroyed by the realization of what will come. We have nothing to look forward to but some cata-clysmic, fated end and whatever unknown future may follow.

The tenth and last section is a meditation on alienation and whole-ness, but it turns again on the question of the meaning of *mal*, or mis-ery, pain, mischance. It reads almost like a theodicy for poetry. An unhappy people in an unhappy world would not be able to define themselves through contrast, nor would a happy people in a happy world. Only an unhappy people in a happy world could provide grist for the imagination's mill, could try to imagine fulfillment. The imag-ined solace is for them no peaceful heaven ("hushful paradise") but a transformed and illumined world brought out of struggle. Opposites are not so much reconciled in this closure as recognized as part of a larger whole in which they have purpose. The thinker, meditating "a whole," confronts and is confronted by his difficult muse and finds the threatening lights of the borealis "like a blaze of summer straw, in win-ter's nick" (*CP*, 421). Opposites are no longer reconciled or "married," but coexist in their full extremity.

"The Auroras of Autumn" is clearer and more logically organized than most of Stevens's long poems, and it echoes in miniature the struc-ture of "Notes toward a Supreme Fiction." But the dominating presence of the mysterious, awe-inspiring lights of the aurora borealis makes this an evening poem, not a poem of daylight. The apocalyptic overtones give the poem a sense of wonder. The end is coming, and this end may or may not be "innocent," but the human imagination continues to operate up to the end despite the minimal light it can produce. Perhaps the ultimate cataclysm will reveal an infinite magnification of the imagination's small light. Stevens's question is always the same. Whatever happens in reality, change or renewal or war or poverty or death, Stevens is always asking, What does poetry do now? How does poetry continue, despite whatever obstacles exist? What does poetry do with this? Is there a grand poem of which each individual poem is a pale and incomplete copy? An Old Testament God is envisioned here, and how can the individual self dare to speak in the presence of the terrifying alien imagination that is this God? We hear the God of Job speaking, asking the poet what on Earth he thought he was doing with language when He, after all, is the Word.

Another evening poem, of a very different tone, is "An Ordinary Evening in New Haven," the other long poem of *The Auroras of Autumn*. Consisting of 31 sections of six tercets each, this lengthy meditation takes an occasion the opposite of that in "The Auroras of Autumn" for its starting point. There are no auroras and no cataclysms; it is, by definition, an "ordinary evening." Stevens commented, "Here my interest is to try to get as close to the ordinary, the commonplace and the ugly as it is possible for a poet to get. It is not a question of grim reality but of plain reality. The object is of course to purge oneself of anything false" (*LWS*, 636). Any revelations in this poem must come from within, not from outside. The energetic casting off of the false and the withered serves as preparation for such an awakening.

"Ordinary Evening" is a hymn to desire, the impulse behind the creation and decreation of fictions. Houses, structures, become major motifs in later Stevens. The structure of one's completed life is tested and interrogated in "To an Old Philosopher in Rome"; the cabin is a major image in "The Auroras of Autumn." The house becomes the completed life, self-built. "Of what is this house composed if not of the sun?" asks the speaker at the beginning of "Ordinary Evening." Of what is a life, a poet's life, composed, if not of reality? This is a major question posed often in Stevens's last poems. He asks, in another poem written during this same period,

> I wonder, have I lived a skeleton's life
> As a disbeliever in reality,
> A countryman of all the bones in the world? (*OP*, 117)

"Ordinary Evening" takes up the self-other, mind-body problem to get at what is mind. "Suppose these houses are composed of ourselves . . . So much ourselves, we cannot tell apart / The idea and the bearer-being of the idea" (*CP*, 466). There is no way to grasp the mind, to observe the self observing, although this is what we desire to do. Beginning from the surface of daily life, this poem probes beneath it to examine the essence of the real. It takes the opposite direction from "The Auroras of Autumn," which begins with the extraordinary and the aberrant, but the destination is the same.

A full-scale discussion of "Ordinary Evening" would be too great a project for this study, but a few of its major concerns can be briefly summarized. Desire is set "deep in the eye," beyond seeing; that is, it is a visceral thing, definable and approachable only in terms of the senses (part 3). The relationship between a demanding, stripping mind and the opaque world is "A responding to a diviner opposite"—there is an accord reached that comes from both sides (part 4). But is it possible to contain world within mind? The belief that it is, that the mind can through its own efforts subsume the world, may be

> . . . disillusion as the last illusion,
> Reality as a thing seen by the mind
> Not that which is but that which is apprehended. (*CP*, 468)

This kind of appropriation would tame reality into a Miltonic pendant world: "A glassy ocean lying at the door / A great town hanging pendant in a shade" (*CP*, 468). To contain reality thus would just be another falsification (part 5). True reality would always be beyond comprehension.

The alternative is couched in mystical terms: "Reality is the beginning not the end, / Naked Alpha, not the hierophant Omega" (*CP*, 469). The cycle is self-renewing (part 6). The major need and focus of our desire is the real: we keep returning to it, away from our fictions of it ("the hotel instead of the hymns / That fall upon it out of the wind" [*CP*, 471]). We want our fiction unmixed with interpretation, a fiction "of pure reality, untouched / by trope or deviation." We do not wish to contain reality but rather to enter it and be contained by it.

> We seek
> Nothing beyond reality. Within it,
> Everything. . . . (part 9; *CP*, 471)

We want to incarnate the real in language, to say it in living terms:

> In the metaphysical streets of the physical town
> We remember the lion of Juda and we save
> The phrase. (*CP*, 472)

But these interpretations cannot last; a phrase like the "lion of Juda" shines with "a nocturnal shine alone," while "The great cat must stand potent in the sun" (*CP*, 473). To use such a phrase is to undermine it (part 11). The lion vanishes like the cat from the fireside in "Montrachet-le-Jardin."

The argument peaks in part 12 with the assertion, "The poem is the cry of its occasion / Part of the res itself and not about it" (*CP*, 473). It is endemic to that particular junction of self and other that can be named "the occasion." It is a part of the present, not the past, and the poet lives within the present and speaks "by sight and insight." "Insight" acquires a second meaning: "in-sight," within vision. An area of whirling leaves is "the area between is and was"; this is the poet's place, to chronicle in words. The exalted tone of this passage crescendos in an "as if" passage that concludes that the "words of the world are the life of the world" (*CP*, 474). It is the poet who vivifies, or animates, his weather by speaking it. But the will or the intention to be spoken must reside in the *res*. There must be a true meeting.

The poem then beats Stevens's usual hasty retreat from extreme assertion and meditates on other means of approaching reality. The ephebe, or student of other poems, is reintroduced, as well as another persona, Professor Eucalyptus of New Haven. The professor seeks "God in the object itself," echoing William Carlos Williams's "no ideas but in things." Instead of "the instinct for heaven," he is dominated by "the instinct for earth." The fulfillment of this desire, the finding of God in things of the world, would translate Earth from an alien to an intimate place. This suggestion recalls "Sunday Morning," but now we are not asked to demythologize, to make the sky "a part of labor and a part of pain" by reclaiming it from God. Rather, we are invited to find the Godhead in the world.

Much of the next few sections consists of a representation of landscape stripped and reduced to the barest minimum. The thinker abstracts the world, and then himself, to get as close as he can to a zero point:

> To have evaded clouds and men leaves him
> A naked being with a naked will
> And everything to make. (*CP*, 480)

But he "may not evade his will"; he cannot see the world straight because his will and "the will of necessity" demand a clothing myth, a "romanza" (*CP*, 480). There are two "romanzas," one of Earth and of the senses, and one representing the total reversal of these. This second myth would be "the opposite of Cythere," Cythere being Baudelaire's promised island of sensory delight that turns out to be nothing but a place of death and rot (*Fleurs*, 66). The opposite island would be a place where the senses "give and nothing take" (*CP*, 480), where the self is poured into the real. These two romanzas speak with a single voice, becoming one story.

Proceeding with Professor Eucalyptus's search for reality, the last third of the poem drifts toward a theory of place as a theory of poetry. New Haven is a place with its own poetic essence, like other places with their weathers. Part 29 was the original conclusion to the poem, and it gives the highest value to language: language alters perception and so, for practical purposes, alters reality:

> . . . an alteration
> Of words that was a change of nature, more
> Than the difference that clouds make over a town.
> The countrymen were changed and each constant thing.
> Their dark-colored words had redescribed the citrons. (*CP*, 487)

The senses and the language called into being by the senses changes the nature of the place; the senses did "give and nothing take."

The revised conclusion places the emphasis not so much on language as on the active effort to approach reality. It is this constant exercise of understanding that is most real, most alive, "edgings and inchings of final form." The process is

> Like an evening evoking the spectrum of violet,
> A philosopher practicing scales on his piano,
> A woman writing a note and tearing it up. (*CP*, 488)

The process of approaching reality is a repetition that seems not to be progress but is: the progress is in the perfecting of the skill. And reality itself is not necessarily impenetrable, not necessarily a solid. "It may be a shade that traverses / A dust, a force that transverses a shade" (*CP*, 489). That is, reality may be process rather than product. It may be a priori, untouchable, beyond definition. Thus does Stevens begin to blur and blend the characteristics of mind and world, so that they partake of as well as mirror each other. They can be seen as one substance.

"A Primitive Like an Orb" shows the extent to which the metaphysical had by this time invaded Stevens's thought and work. About this poem, Joseph Carroll comments, "The purpose of this poem is to expound the basic idea of [Stevens's] supreme fiction, the idea that the poet's individual fictions derive from and reflect essential imagination, that is, the world-creating mind of God" (260). Carroll points out that "A Primitive" suggests the subman of "Owl's Clover," whereas the orb "serves as a geometric figuration for the universal whole that is a construct of the speculative reason" (261). He recalls Stevens's reference to Pascal, whom Stevens believed to have described God as "la sphère dont le centre est partout et la circonférence est nulle part" (the circle whose center is everywhere and whose circumference is nowhere) (*OP*, 94; Carroll, 262).[5]

"A Primitive," like Stevens's other late credo poems, is formal in structure, consisting of 12 numbered eight-line stanzas of blank verse. Its movement is between the "essential poem at the centre of things" (*CP*, 440) of its first line and the "lesser poems" in which the central poem is found. The first section has the slightest tinge of Stevens's invented professoriat of "Extracts from the Academy of Fine Ideas": the "dear sirs" are lectured to the effect that there are serious limitations placed on the apperception of the central poem. Our ability to touch and be touched by this underlying good is present, but limited by ability and circumstance. The "gold" that is "fortune's finding" is "disposed and re-disposed / By such slight genii in such pale air" (*CP*, 440).

The audience disappears as the poem becomes direct and intense, describing how the central poem informs lesser poems without being visible as itself. The poem is a poetic prime mover, source and substance of the individual poems that come from it.

> It is the huge, high harmony that sounds
> A little and a little, suddenly,
> By means of a separate sense. (*CP*, 440)

The poem is the ghost in the machine, the spirit that informs the letter, the music of the spheres. A preparation for celebration is described ("Green guests and table in the woods" [*CP*, 440]), and a heightened sense of possibility is present in this sacrament of participation in the world. The fourth section evokes Shakespeare's fantasizers as described by Theseus in *Midsummer Night's Dream*: lunatic, lover, and poet, substituting "believer" for "lunatic" (Carroll, 269) and thus inverting Theseus's dismissal of fantasy into an invocation to it. These believers and practitioners are "clairvoyant"; for them the world's opacities are transparent.

The fourth, fifth, and sixth sections suggest that a progressive unveiling occurs through poetry, as poets with "words . . . chosen out of their desire / The joy of language . . . celebrate the central poem" (*CP*, 441). The first half of the poem ends with a resounding affirmation: "The essential poem begets the others. The light / Of it is not a light apart, up-hill" (*CP*, 441). The last six stanzas constitute a hymn to the central poem, investing it with the mystical significance of Dante's Paradiso. It is "the poem of the composition of the whole," and it is "the roundness that pulls tight the final ring" (*CP*, 442). The central poem is a sentience, "A giant on the horizon, glistening" (*CP*, 442). The images of ultimate exaltation are piled up as the giant becomes a king, "vested in the serious folds of majesty." The poem evolves the giant, "an abstraction given head," reminiscent of the "abstraction blooded" of "Chocorua to Its Neighbor." But here what is being stressed may be less the giant's elusiveness than its power. It is imagination imagining itself, that which human beings cannot do. It is a "grave / And prodigious person, patron of origins" (*CP*, 443).

The last section retreats to the individual human imaginers—the lover, the believer, and the poet—and describes their role as part of this essential poem:

> Each one, his fated eccentricity,
> As a part, but part, the tenacious particle,
> Of the skeleton of the ether, the total
> Of letters, prophesies, perceptions. . . . (*CP*, 443)

The giant of the weather is more fully glimpsed and affirmed than in the earlier poems, and he is more alive: "the giant ever changing, living in change" (*CP*, 443).

In one way or another, most of the poems in *The Auroras of Autumn* celebrate the "necessary angel" that Stevens celebrates in his poem "Angel Surrounded by Paysans," which concludes the collection and from which he took the title to his collection of essays. The poem was inspired by a painting by Tal Coat that Stevens had purchased—as he usually did—without seeing first. Entitled "Still Life," the painting

includes a Venetian glass bowl—the "angel"—that dominates a surrounding group of bottles and glasses. A statement Stevens made about
the picture might have a bearing on the poem. "For all its in-door light
on in-door objects, the picture refreshes one with an out-door sense of
things," he wrote (*LWS*, 649). And, in fact, the angel is the crosser of
thresholds, the bringer of light from one world to another.

The poem mocks the traditional angel apparatus as a cliché; the angel
announces, "I have neither ashen wing nor wear of ore / And live without a tepid aureole" (*CP*, 496). His function is nevertheless angelic; his
annunciation is the reality of the world and its renewal. His vision is to
refresh, to make visible the world as it is, without its falsifications.

> I am the necessary angel of earth
> Since in my sight, you see the earth again,
> Cleared of its stiff and stubborn, man-locked set. (*CP*, 496)

Muse of earth, this angel's task is to strip away the fake and demonstrate
the truth of the real. But toward the end of the poem, he changes,
acquiring angelic properties that come close to the "wing" and "aureole"
he scorns. He asks if he is not "only half of a figure of a sort"—a liminal
form that is not quite corporeal, and if he is not

> . . . an apparition appareled in
> Apparels of such lightest look that a turn
> Of my shoulder and quickly, I am gone? (*CP*, 497)

"Angel of earth" notwithstanding, he is an angel, and it is his purpose to
console, to heal, and to allow glimpses of otherness into the faded ordinary, as is generally the function of divine messengers. With this enigmatic annunciation, Stevens concludes his collection.

Chapter Seven

"The Celestial Possible":
Last Poems

Stevens kept up a hectic pace with his dual career well into his seventies. As an internationally acclaimed poet who had received nearly all the major awards, including the National Book Award and the coveted Bollingen Prize, he had far more demands on his time than he could possibly meet. Universities were eager to give him honorary degrees; writers and editors kept after him to write prefaces and reviews. He had to be selective, especially since he did not have the energy he once had. Perhaps surprisingly, his major fear was that the Hartford would ask him to retire. Retirement was mandatory at 70, and many executives retired before then. But Stevens kept requesting and receiving annual dispensations from the retirement age. He had no need to keep working and could easily have spent the rest of his time on poetry. But he chose not to. Thus, when Archibald MacLeish wrote in November 1954 to ask him to be the Charles Eliot Norton Professor at Harvard for the following year, he refused, on the grounds that "to take the greater part of a year . . . for something else would be only too likely to precipitate the retirement that I want so much to put off" (*LWS*, 853). At the end of his life, he had little communication with Elsie, who continued to spend most of her time gardening, taking care of the house, and living in her suite while he kept to his. Holly was his companion for rare literary evenings. Each day, he worked in the office, worked on his poetry, and went to bed very early instead of reading and writing into the night as he once had.

By the time he wrote to MacLeish, he must have already been feeling the onset of his final illness. He dated his symptoms from January 1955, when his wife had a stroke and he altered his own lifestyle to accommodate the needs of an invalid in the house. He did not visit a physician until March, thinking that the change in habits was causing his indigestion and other problems. When he did, a battery of tests showed intestinal obstruction. Exploratory surgery done on 26 April at St. Francis Hospital showed advanced cancer. Since his case was clearly terminal, the doctor performed a gastroenterostomy above the cancer to alleviate the obstruction. Stevens was not told of the diagnosis. Sent home to recover from the operation, he insisted on going back to work at the office almost immediately, although it was obvious to his coworkers that he was in serious pain. On 31 July he was readmitted to the hospital, and he died there on 2 August. Visitors commented on how relaxed and even content he seemed in the hospital; one friend said, "He was the most capable in knowing how to die" (Brazeau, 292). But not until 20 years later was it revealed to a partly disbelieving coterie of scholars that, during his last illness, he had taken instruction for, and finally become a member of, the Roman Catholic Church.

Stevens's baptism at the hospital into Catholicism has been flatly denied by some and explained away by others as whim or coercion; still others have made his conversion the basis for a reinterpretation of his work.[1] Its factuality has been attested to by Father Arthur Hanley, who visited with Stevens during his last illness. "He often remarked about the peace and tranquility that he experienced in going into a Catholic Church and spending some time," Father Hanley wrote in 1977, subsequent to a long telephone conversation with this author and Beverly Coyle about the conversion. "He spoke about St. Patrick's Cathedral in New York."[2] According to Hanley, he baptized Stevens at the hospital after about ten sessions of instruction and discussion. In a taped interview with Peter Brazeau, the priest noted that the conversion took place over a period of months and involved discussion with others besides himself (Brazeau, 294). Stevens's baptism, then, was not a deathbed impulse. Others have testified to Stevens's interest in religion, but only Father Hanley remained alive in the 1970s to bear witness to the fact of the poet's baptism as a Roman Catholic. Hanley died in 1992. In his last years, he felt so beset by questions concerning Stevens's conversion that he was reluctant to answer any more of them.[3]

The publicizing of Stevens's conversion has resulted in rereadings as well as in controversy. The strong preoccupation of his 1950s work with metaphysical concerns is clear. The direction taken by *The Auroras of Autumn* is continued in the poems of "The Rock," the last section of *The Collected Poems*, and in other late poems not included in that volume (either because Stevens had not written them in time or because he chose not to include them). To experience the transcendent vision of Stevens's late work, one need only listen to the Caedmon recording made in 1954. The selection of poems that court the infinite and intermingle images of conclusions and beginnings, with incidental church bells in the background, is a powerful argument.[4] The poems chosen for the reading are not all late poems or metaphysical poems, but their overall effect is of a credo.

In a sense, the poems of "The Rock" may be considered an epilogue. In their summation of what it means to have been a poet, to have made poetry one's motivating force and major lifework, they veer in two opposing directions, toward metaphysics and toward despondency. The more optimistic poems find a cosmic sanction for poetry, whereas the more pessimistic efforts see only the ending of the life of poetic effort. Often, however, Stevens begins in a mood of apparent dejection at the seeming futility of the poetic endeavor, which he sometimes compares with the construction of a building, but then he is taken over by the positive impulse. Thus, he alters to some extent his earlier direction of following every affirmation with a hasty retreat, thereby concluding many poems and the collection itself on an affirmative note.

"Prologues to What Is Possible" exemplifies Stevens's late explorative mode. In its search for a new definition of metaphysics, "Prologues" alludes to the Jungian collective unconscious. It also typifies the late poems in its mingling of elegy and exaltation. The poem is about metaphor and could almost be considered an embodiment of Jung's description of metaphor, which he identifies as an expression of an archetypal content: "If such a content should speak of the sun and identify it with the lion, the king, the hoard of gold guarded by the dragon, or the power that makes for the life and health of man, it is neither the one thing nor the other, but the unknown third thing that finds more or less adequate expression in all those similes, yet—to the vexation of the intellect—remains unknown and not to be fitted into a formula."[5]

"Prologues" is controlled by several archetypes. The voyager is the seer who evolves toward the possible self and the self of the race. Ancient cultures distinguished between the "lower waters" (what exists) and the "upper waters" (what is still possible); the journey crosses from one to the other in its evolution. The voyage toward reality or wholeness is undertaken in a stone boat; stone in Stevens is wholeness, combining the opposites of basis and finality. The fire of the boat's "speculum" is consciousness. In the poem, consciousness is being transformed by experience as each "flick" makes permanent changes in the perceiver. "Prologues" is also a demonstration of the methods of poetry. Its transitions of thought are represented by shifts that violate our expectations of metaphor and ultimately convert figurative language into direct statement.

Initially, "an ease of mind" is compared to "being alone in a boat at sea," but the waves carrying the boat then become the tenor of another metaphor, the vehicle of which is "the bright backs of rowers" (*CP*, 515). Through flowing, fleeting comparisons, thought becomes action. With the swiftness of rushing water, the scene moves from mind to world, and back to mind again, as the rowers move "as if they were sure of their destination" (*CP*, 515). The impression of motion is increased by the number of participles used—such as "gripping," "bending," "pulling"—as the reader is pulled into the rapidly moving vehicle of the poem. But the forward movement is balanced by the speaker's retreat from his subject: he takes one step backward with each "as if." Thus, there are simultaneous movements, away from the shore, outward from the subject through layers of metaphor, and inward toward the center that is the mind's true destination.

The second part of the first section continues the motion, but now the movement is calmed or contained. The relative peace is suggested by "glided" and "glass-like." That this is a voyage inward is apparent from its destination, "a point of central arrival," from which the speaker remains estranged, however, by "like" and "as." The boat, like Stevens's other symbols of the mind, is a vessel of light. It is made of weightless, brilliant stones, and the "speculum of fire" on its prow combines mirror and lamp. Reality, the center about which all metaphors cluster, the unsymbolized symbol, is "syllable without any meaning" and yet simultaneously "the meaning he wanted to enter" (*CP*, 516).

Part 2 expounds the metaphor introduced in part 1, allowing the metaphor to gloss itself. Becoming aware of his position, the man in the boat is frightened by it. He knows that he is not in control of his journey, and that his knowledge of self and other is severely limited. Universal analogy overwhelms him.

> The metaphor stirred his fear. The object with
>   which he was compared
> Was beyond his recognizing. By this he knew
>   that likeness of himself extended
> Only a little way, and not beyond, unless between himself
> And things beyond resemblance there was this and
>   that to be recognized,
> The this and that in the enclosures of hypotheses
> On which men speculated in summer when they were half asleep. (*CP*, 516)

His self-awareness, paradoxically, puts him back into the natural world. The gap between mind and world has been bridged, not by affirming the one at the expense of the other but by recognizing their kinship (or even their identity).

The movement of the first section of part 2 is a spreading out from the individual self toward the collective and universal, but the second section shifts back to the self as the poet explains the effect that discovery of the collective has on the individual. Discovery of the likeness between self and world brings out the possibility of finding new diversity within the mind itself: "What self, for example, did he contain that had not yet been loosed / Snarling in him for discovery as his attentions spread" (*CP*, 516). Anything is possible for the voyager who recognizes possibility. The last two sections of part 2 combine the parallel themes of the inward and outward journeys into one movement, described in images of light. The new awareness of the boatman opens outward into infinite possibility.

The light of the mind, reintegrated with the collective unconscious ("his hereditary lights"), is changed and increased. The traveler marks the change with words and gives it a name to complete the poetic process. The "puissant flick" is compared in the last section of part 2 with changes in the natural world. The effect of the addition to the mind parallels the change made in the world by "the earliest single light in the evening sky, in spring," which "creates a fresh universe . . . by adding itself" (*CP*, 517). The concluding passage recalls Stevens's notion of place as defining identity and combines images of light with images of words, sounds, and meanings. The point of central arrival is that place where word, flesh, and mind meld into one, identity being the vanishing point of resemblance.

"Prologues" is only one example of epiphany in Stevens's last phase. His work, as he arranged it on the seasonal cycle, concludes with spring renewal rather than winter death, although it is a tentative, unusual renewal compared with the familiar budding out of his earlier springs. The two movements of Stevens's poetry, the cycle of seasons and the "voyaging . . . up and down between two elements," become one in a spiraling toward the center. The spiral motion replaces the simple cycle of *Harmonium*.

There is also a new solidity to some of these late poems. The total product that represents a life's achievement, or perhaps an achieved life, is often described as a building. Stevens's attitude toward these buildings varies, however; in one poem about an old man, he observes that "the great structure has become a minor house" (*CP*, 502), whereas in another poem of another old man he speaks of the "total grandeur of a total

edifice" (*CP*, 510). In "Saint Armorer's Church from the Outside," the
new chapel replaces the old destroyed church, like a new spring growth,
"an ember yes among its cindery noes" (*CP*, 529). The "up and down" in
these poems is not between his two familiar compass points of north and
south, but between positive and negative valuation of the poetic act and
of the meaning of consciousness itself (the candle flame). Another "up
and down" is a wavering between despair at the prospect of total loss
and joy in a possible rebirth of consciousness.

Among Stevens's late poems, only a few are frequently anthologized;
one work popular with anthologists is "To an Old Philosopher in Rome."
This valedictory poem takes the final days of Stevens's old mentor from
Harvard, George Santayana, as occasion for a meditation on the completed life of the mind. A 1935 *New Yorker* essay described the circumstances of Santayana's last days in a hospital in Rome; Stevens must have
been struck particularly by the descriptions of the nurses' hats, which
stood out from their heads like immense paper boats.[6] Before any indica-
tion of his conversion to Catholicism had surfaced, Lucy Beckett commented, "Stevens is here very near to a spiritual centre, a point of rest,
that could well be described in the traditional terms of Christian theolo-
gy" (186).

"To an Old Philosopher" bids farewell to the structure of the mind's
creation, which is seen from the perspective of the departing thinker.
Santayana may have represented for Stevens the rational philosopher
whose systematic understanding of the world maintains its integrity
despite challenge. The poem uses a formal structure of 16 five-line stanzas of relaxed iambic pentameter in its representation of the architecture
of the mental life. The "threshold of heaven" from which the old philosopher looks is the doorway of his departure from life, that liminal crossing
that allows a kind of seepage from one world to another. From this perspective, what he sees is mixed with what he imagines, "the figures in
the street /   become the figures of heaven." The sights and sounds of
Rome become for him those of "that more merciful Rome / Beyond,"
although these two are "alike in the make of the mind" (*CP*, 508).
"Make" carries two senses, "creation" and the more archaic "companion"
or "lover." It is as if—the transcendent suggestion is made, but only as a
hypothesis—there were some larger vision in which the real city of Rome
and the imagined Holy City are one.

The poem blurs the real and the imagined in representing the mind of
the dying philosopher, who sees familiar scenes as if touched with the
strangeness of a revelation: "In a confusion on bed and books, a portent /

On the chair, a moving transparence on the nuns." The flickering consciousness of the old thinker desiring and intuiting freedom from the confines of a self is suggested by the

> . . . light on the candle tearing against the wick
> To join a hovering excellence, to escape
> From fire and be part only of that of which
> Fire is the symbol: the celestial possible. (*CP*, 509)

Flame = consciousness = the possibility of cosmic consciousness. God is manifested as the creating Mind.

The poem does retreat from this precipice, though, in Stevens's familiar way: to name the magical is still to dispel it. The celestial possible remains just that: a possibility. The focus returns to the philosopher, who is the subject of our pity and admiration as, within his humane and humanistic philosophy, he barely clings to life. The observers of the philosopher identify with him in his vulnerability, the magnificence of his enterprise, and the realization that the human condition does not allow one a view beyond it. Reality, or at least what we take for reality, is "poverty." And thus its language is most ours: "It is poverty's speech that seeks us out the most. / It is older than the oldest speech of Rome" (*CP*, 510).

The dying philosopher thus inhabits the structure of his room, the world he has created and illuminated. His life at its conclusion, as achievement arrives at closure, is touched with magnificence. It is changed and yet it is not changed.

> It is a kind of total grandeur at the end,
>
> With every visible thing enlarged and yet
> No more than a bed, a chair and moving nuns,
> The immensest theatre, the pillared porch,
> The book and candle in your ambered room. . . . (*CP*, 510)

A kind of sanctification has taken place, the mental energy of the thinker investing his mind's creation with life. At the end, there is a pause:

> He stops upon this threshold,
> As if the design of all his words takes form
> And frame from thinking and is realized. (*CP*, 511)

In leaving the life of the mind, it is as if the structure of his thought has come into existence—as if the mental building that the thinker conceived and lived in had become "real." It is as if energetic and lifelong commitment to the interrogation of structures allowed one to alter reality with the mind and voice. This is a much more intense and personal poem than "The Idea of Order at Key West," which suggests some of the same ideas but more implicitly as well as more tentatively.

The centerpiece poem, "The Rock," presents an equivocal judgment on the poet's ultimate meaning and value. Composed of three sections of nine, eleven, and seven three-line stanzas of iambic pentameter, it is a subdued, meditative, summing-up poem. The first section, "Seventy Years Later," describes a life from the perspective of age. (Stevens was 70 when he wrote the poem.) "The Poem as Icon" focuses on the meaning of art; "Forms of the Rock as a Night-Hymn" focuses on the nature of reality, or the human experience of reality. The third part does in a generalized and abstract way what is done on a more personal level in part 1.

To roughly summarize the poem's argument: From the perspective of 70 years, youthful freedom seems to have been an illusion. There is only a husk left of this imagined freedom. The first 12 lines express a perplexed sense of loss: the past has not merely gone away, but it never was. "The sounds of the guitar / Were not and are not. Absurd" (*CP*, 525). "Absurd" strikes the dissonant chord of the present truth that gives the lie to memory. The freedom of the past seems to have been a fiction, invented by "two figures in a nature of the sun / In the sun's design of its own happiness" (*CP*, 525). The two did not live their own lives, create their own scene, but instead lived in the design of the sun, within the purposes of another and an alien reality.

From here, the husks of houses and the atmosphere of futility disappear. Self-determination may have disappeared, but not determination. It is true that, as so often, Stevens's assertions are qualified by the "as if," but it is important to remember that Stevens did not intend his qualifications to signify that certain statements are untrue, but simply that they describe appearances. The reality they may represent cannot be proved.

It appears, then, that the design comes from the perceived world and not from the perceiver, from the other and not from the self:

> As if nothingness contained a métier,
> A vital assumption, an impermanence
> In its permanent cold, an illusion so desired
>
> That the green leaves came and covered the high rock. . . . (*CP*, 526)

Chaos thus contains order and intends the manifestations of the visible world. The assertion may be undercut by the use of the French *métier* (career), with the irony that emerges in the notion of giving nothingness an occupation. But basically, this is an active mysticism. The "green leaves" are the product of a stronger imagination than that of the meditative Snow Man, who saw the "nothing that is not there and the nothing that is." The emphasis passes from the observer to the observed, and the imagination is shared and self-generating; it is something beyond the self. The rock itself is the basis of the imagination. The concluding lines of "Seventy Years Later" contain no agent; the vatic *we* has disappeared.

"The Poem as Icon" takes up these questions: If the purpose, or the meaning, belongs to reality and not to the individual perceiver, and if we cannot decipher this meaning, then what is art? How can we heal the sense of alienation that comes from the incompleteness of our vision? Such a healing would be hypothetical, and attempts at a poetry of healing would produce hypothetical poems. The icon is a representation of a sacred person and is also sacred in itself. Thus, it is valued both for what it is and for what it represents. Stevens's icon is his "copy of the sun," his copy of reality, which is for him divinity. The religious imagery equates rather than compares poetry with religion and describes a sacrament by which the poet can share the substance of the rock—eating the "incipient colorings" of the leaves the rock produces in its manifestation of otherness.

> It is not enough to cover the rock with leaves.
> We must be cured of it by a cure of the ground
> Or a cure of ourselves, that is equal to a cure
>
> Of the ground, a cure beyond forgetfulness.
> And yet the leaves, if they broke into bud,
> If they broke into bloom, if they bore fruit,
>
> And if we ate the incipient colorings
> Of their fresh culls might be a cure of the ground. (*CP*, 526)

This nature eucharist is an attempt at healing and restoration, in fact, at salvation: "a cure beyond forgetfulness," that is, a cure that would negate death. "Cure" itself has the double meaning of preserving and establishing health. The sacrament is a mystical participation in nature that takes away its otherness and heals the great split between mind and world. The sacrament reflects the difficulty of this healing. To eat the "incipient colorings" of the "fresh culls" would be to subsume past and future in the present. "Culls" are plants picked and set aside as inferior. The culls are pasts, while "incipient colorings" are futures. If we could contain past and future in our experience of the present, then we would comprehend time within us and be free of it. Intriguingly, in the middle of "The Poem as Icon," the tense changes from the conditional to the direct: "They bud and bloom . . . They are more than leaves" (*CP*, 527). The whole structure of the hypothesis depends on (or derives from) an initial "if," but because of the shift to direct active, the entire set of possibilities takes on the vivid life of a believed fiction.

The lines beginning "The fiction of the leaves is the icon" provide a series of equivalences that describe the healing, or cure: leaves = icon = poem = seasons = man. The interchangeability of these terms creates the final fiction. The "fictions of the leaves" are not invented worlds, but real ones. In other words, the copying or creation has been done by nature itself. "Time's autumn snood" is "its copy of the sun" because, although the sun is timeless, autumn provides a specific manifestation of its power. If the breach between self and other were healed, the man would be the rock, and the blooming and change would be introjected. The leaves are no longer part of the rock alone but are of the feeling and the senses. This union is the "final found, / The plenty of the year and of the world" (*CP*, 527). It is discovery, not invention.

"Forms of the Rock in a Night-Hymn" discusses the rock as actually perceived but without the "cure." The second section describes the rock in sunlight, the light of reality, and the discussion must then be conjectural because our light is the light of the mind. Therefore, the second part is full of "as ifs," whereas the last part is closer to flat statement. The tone is elegiac, and the earlier exaltation is gone. The contrast may suggest the pathos of the gap between what is and what might be; we might have had "copies of the sun" but have instead only "night-hymns." In this section, the rock no longer contains and engenders all things but becomes one thing at a time. It has forms. No longer merely gray, it is red or turquoise depending on the position of the observer. We cannot penetrate the rock's surface, but we can use it as an astrolabe. Even within the constraints given, much is possible.

In the last stanzas, the focus moves back from the imperviousness of the rock to man to the nature of the rock itself. Although the meditator cannot penetrate the rock, it contains all. Individual experience is measured as an arc against the rock's full circle; an individual mortal life, the mango's rind, represents two definite points against the seamless surface.

The conclusion is made difficult by the grammatical ambiguity of the passage.

> It is the rock where tranquil must adduce
> Its tranquil self, the main of things, the mind,
>
> The starting point of the human and the end,
> That in which space itself is contained, the gate
> To the enclosure, day, the things illumined
>
> By day, night, and that which night illumines,
> Night and its midnight-minting fragrances,
> Night's hymn of the rock, as in a vivid sleep. (*CP*, 528)

The list of things following "adduce" may all be objects of "adduce," or they may not. "Adduce" means to bring forth as evidence, to justify through evidence. If all the listed items are intended as objects of "adduce," then the sentence may mean that the rock of reality provides the parameters by which the mind measures its worlds, and these measurements become a hymn in praise of the rock itself. The rock is seen as in a "vivid sleep": it is vital or vivid, and yet sleeping because our perception is so limited as to make all our waking life a sleep.

Many of Stevens's last poems share this hint at rebirth, this rebirth into another plane of existence so altered as to require a different language. In "The Rock," an old man reviews his life and compares two possible perspectives, a known rational one by which his experience was illusion, and a hypothetical, irrational one by which it was real. Then he asks, If our perspective is the rational one, by which experience is illusory, then what is art? The answer is that in art we seek the other perspective. We force reason to go beyond itself; we peer beyond the limits of our vision. If we are not successful, we nevertheless hold before ourselves by this means the possibility of transcendence.

Stevens never abandoned his major declaration that "the gods come out of the weather." But now he infuses the numinous into place in its broadest sense; it would almost seem that the weather comes out of the gods. Two late poems of departure, "On the Way to the Bus" and "As You Leave the Room," are tentative descriptions of a cycle in which *logos* becomes not an imposition of man but an inherent quality of being: the world speaks itself in its own language. Its dialogue may be heard, or overheard. Its message is a revelation. Those intrigued by Stevens's deathbed conversion may read the message as revelation itself, although it is hard to read these poems as monolithically optimistic. They advance in fits and starts toward a conclusive affirmation.

Of these two, the more straightforward is "As You Leave the Room," a poem that may have been written in 1944 and reworked in 1955. It is a reflective retrospection, uncharacteristically personal, in which the speaker wonders if he has after all truly lived: "I wonder, have I lived a skeleton's life / As a disbeliever in reality?" (*OP*, 117). It is "the snow I had forgotten," this realization of transience in which the wise man builds his city, that makes him aware that he has in fact lived a real life. His refusal to compromise his vision has actualized his life to the extent that it has made it seem as though he could take his vision with him, a reification of perception. It is, he says, "as if I left / With something I could touch, touch every way." But the irony is that what has given him his reality and persuaded him of his own existence is the unreal: "And yet nothing has been changed except what is / Unreal, as if nothing had been changed at all" (*OP*, 118). The unreal, then, has a being, for something has in fact been changed. The poem suggests that life is one of those dreams in which the dreamer, knowing that he is asleep, clutches the dream-gift against dawn, hoping against hope that he will not lose it. And yet it also suggests the possibility that this gift of self, this miraculous imagination, may somehow be kept.

The other poem is preoccupied with a similar question. That the true poetry is not the poem had been established from Stevens's earliest writing. Poetry is the willed act of vision that remakes both seer and seen. What, then, happens when the poetic act is concluded? "On the Way to the Bus" also suggests imminent departure by its title (which implies an arrival as well). Here too the snow is present, and it is "like frost," frost being one of Stevens's death images. This weather brings the "journalist" to the awareness that there comes from cold "an understanding beyond journalism." This understanding would be an endemic poetry, a poetry that is truly inherent in the speaker, "A way of pronouncing the word inside of one's tongue" (*OP*, 136). This perfection is not available to the journalist, but it exists: it must be possible for a human being to speak the word that he was born to speak. "Journalism" would be debased description, a reduction of the truth. The coming cold sharpens the eye.

In addition to their speculation about the meaning of having been a poet, Stevens's last poems repeatedly ask the final epistemological questions. What if the final veil that remains between observer and observed even after the most rigorous scrutiny were removed? Would there then be no gap between the mind and the world? Would the world be experienced as mind? And finally, would this experience be the knowledge of God? "We say that God and the imagination are one," Stevens says in "Final Soliloquy of the Interior Paramour." "How high that highest candle lights the dark" (*CP*, 524). The image of the candle itself is an image of centeredness, and while the passage is usually taken to mean that imagination is God, it might as readily be taken to mean what it says: that God *is* imagination, or that the real and imagined world is the manifestation of God's presence. In "Presence of an External Master of Knowledge," he takes up this possibility as a direct hypothesis; in other poems, he suggests it.

Four poems written too late for *The Collected Poems* appeared as a numbered series in the *Sewanee Review*. Each follows a similar pattern, beginning with a negation and working through to a tentative affirmation. As a group and individually, these poems suggest that there may exist a center where making and finding are one, and that this center is a transcendence. The four poems are "Solitaire under the Oaks," "Local Objects," "Artificial Populations," and "A Clear Day and No Memories." The poems demonstrate the process whereby the mind contemplates the world, fails to contain it, yields to it instead, and finds as a result a sense of fulfillment, a mystical participation that cannot be defined. A brief discussion of two of the poems will suffice to demonstrate.

In "Solitaire under the Oaks," the title suggests a contrast between two aspects of the world: the natural and sense-bound (oaks) and the abstract and mathematical (solitaire). The solitaire also suggests the individual consciousness. In the poem, the sense of the isolated self is diminished by the odd combination of randomness and design in nature: "In the oblivion of cards / One exists among pure principles" (*OP*, 137). Perhaps a recognition of design superimposes itself on the sense of individual isolation usually experienced by the solitary card player, and he senses the presence of the abstract:

> Neither the cards nor the trees nor the air
> Persist as facts. This is an escape
>
> To principium. . . . (OP, 137)

"Principium" is ultimate foundation, ultimate cause; freed from the particular, the mind is released to the abstract and becomes part of it. "One knows at last what to think about," the speaker continues, suggesting a quiet revelation; one "thinks about it without consciousness / . . . completely released" (OP, 137). The message is Zen-like: through contemplation of structures without content—the numbers, the formal sets—the mind is released into the nothing that is something. The release is an escape from the prison of self. It is significant that the individual must be alone to experience such a revelation. The self becomes so absorbed that the barriers are down and the natural meanings and intentions of the world can be felt.

"Artificial Populations" also begins with a negative statement, but this time the statement is qualified immediately and without apology.

> The centre that he sought was a state of mind,
> Nothing more, like weather after it has cleared—
> Well, more than that, like weather when it has cleared
> And the two poles continue to maintain it. . . . (OP, 138)

The center sought is, in fact, more than "a state of mind"; it is more like a clarity of vision, the result of being operated on by outside forces.

> And the Orient and the Occident embrace
> To form that weather's appropriate people,
> The rosy men and women of the rose,
> Astute in being what they are made to be. (OP, 138)

The tension of the opposites after the clearing of the weather produces what the "centre" is like—it is like the "appropriate people" of the cleared weather, the men and women of the rose. The landscape-defined populations of earlier poems, including the "pine-spokesman" of "The Comedian as the Letter C," have developed a new dimension. The rose itself is a symbol of the mystical at the heart of the physical. This population, although "artificial," does not come from the seeker's artifice but from the tension of opposites, the two poles that represent all of Stevens's antitheses, male and female, sun and moon, mind and world.

This is another *hieros gamos*, or mystic-marriage image, like those in his earlier poems; it brings to mind in particular "Winter and spring, cold copulars, embrace, / And forth the particulars of rapture come" (*CP*, 392). This particular marriage, though, implies both intentionality on the part of the poles ("what they are made to be") and sentience on the part of the created ("astute"). This "population" is like

> A healing-point in the sickness of the mind:
> Like angels resting on a rustic steeple
> Or a confect of leafy faces in a tree. . . . (*OP*, 138)

"Artificial Populations" contains one of Stevens's series of opening similes. The center is a state of mind that is like cleared weather in which tension and intention of opposites produces that weather's people. These people are like the healing-point, which is like angels or leafy faces. Thus, through a series of analogues, absence has become charged with presence, and we have passed from the nothing of cleared weather through men and women to angels. The image of angels resting on a steeple recalls the scholastic conundrum: How many angels can stand on the head of a pin? An infinity of them, or none at all? Can the incorporeal produce the corporal? The result of all these transformations is

> A health—and the faces in a summer night.
> So too, of the races of appropriate people
> Of the wind, of the wind as it deepens, and late sleep,
> And music that lasts long and lives the more. (*OP*, 138)

The mind's sickness is healed by "peopling" its most important objects— a concept Stevens develops elsewhere, in his "an abstraction blooded," for instance. Like others in the group, this poem describes the relationship of mind to things of nature as including a numinous quality and locates that quality neither in the mind nor in the world but in the act of perception. The "state of mind" that is introduced so deprecatingly at the beginning becomes all-important as perception turns into creation.

Because Stevens's last poems often still exhibit his typical pattern of asserting a position and then undercutting it, because he still hides behind masks, critics can easily focus on only those poems that support their theses about where Stevens's work ends up. But the assertions of the last poems are more extreme and more positive than those in earlier poems, and what is finally claimed is the most anyone can claim for poetry: that it is intended, that it comes from outside its human creator. These poems head toward a closure, and that final point where opposites rest in concord is an identity, that vanishing point of resemblance, of mind and world.

Two poems more explicit than others are "Presence of an External Master of Knowledge" and "A Child Asleep in Its Own Life." These were published together less than a year before Stevens's death and were probably written shortly before publication. That he chose not to include them in his *Collected Poems* does not suggest that he disclaimed their premises but may mean that he recognized their explicitness, as he did that of the poems in *Owl's Clover*. They do not

> . . . make the visible a little hard
> To see, nor reverberating, eke out the mind
> On peculiar horns. (*CP*, 311).

Therefore, they are not in his view the best poetry.

"Presence of an External Master of Knowledge" is as transparent as the world Ulysses inhabits. This poem is a telescoped version of "The Sail of Ulysses"; "A Child Asleep in Its Own Life" is also taken from the long poem. "The Sail of Ulysses" was a long poem Stevens wrote to deliver at the Phi Beta Kappa exercises at Columbia in 1954, but he was not satisfied with the poem, finding it too general and perhaps even too revealing. At one point he wrote, "I shall certainly never use it in its present form nor allow anyone to see a copy of it" (*LWS*, 845). Stevens may have believed that, by cutting out the more grandiose statements, he could save the poem, but he finally decided that even the more cryptic version was too explicit. The title of "External Master" heralds the presence of the other mind. Ulysses, "symbol of the seeker," has found what he has long sought. At last he knows reality, and it knows him. He speaks, saying the words it intends for him to say.

> "Here I feel the human loneliness
> And that, in space and solitude,
> Which knowledge is: the world and fate,
> The right within me and about me,
> Joined in a triumphant vigor,
> Like a direction on which I depend. . . ." (*OP*, 131)

Ulysses has come to his meeting not with the faithful Penelope of Stevens's other poem about Ulysses but with the other, unmediated and without form. Now "knowing and being are one," and Ulysses has earned his knowledge and recognition. He announces, "The great Omnium descends on me, / Like an absolute out of this eloquence."

> After this gift, the sail of Ulysses is literally inspired:
> The sharp sail of Ulysses seemed,
> In the breathings of that soliloquy,
> Alive with an enigma's flittering. . . . (*OP*, 132)

Although the element of uncertainty remains in the words *seemed* and *like*, the poem implies a fated meeting with the outside imaginer, and this fatality remains with the conclusion that "he moved, straightly, on and on / Through clumped stars dangling all the way" (*OP*, 132). Beyond the human imagination is the inhuman imagination, its mirror and creator.

"A Child Asleep in Its Own Life" takes its title from "The Sail of Ulysses," in which the line appears as part of a list of possibilities for "the sibyl's shape" (*OP*, 104). The poem is short, consisting of three unrhymed tercets. There is "one" among the "old men that you know" who "broods / On all the rest" (*OP*, 132). The "you" addressed is the sleeping child. The "unnamed" old man's power extends over all the rest, for he is "the sole emperor of what they are." He is not, however, the emperor of ice-cream; he is the emperor of mind, and his dominion extends everywhere. He is "distant" and yet "close enough to wake / The chords above your bed to-night" (*OP*, 132). The images of the poem may suggest the kind of farewell pictured in the cartoons of the old year passing on the banner to the new, but there is no suggestion of the imminent extinction of the old man: he is there, and the universe exists in his head. The wisdom of his single mind informs. He may also be an external master of knowledge, but humanized.

Is Stevens's external master of knowledge human in any sense? Stevens's acceptance of Catholic Christianity at the end suggests a preference for divinity with a human dimension, but many of the last poems (not including "The Sail of Ulysses" and the shorter poems derived from it) look to a form of knowledge that seems alien and inhuman. In fact, the tone of resignation of some of these poems seems to derive not from the idea that his world is ending but from the sense that the new language to be spoken is incomprehensible, is not his language. Reality speaks its own language; there is a communication from which he is excluded.

This sense of exclusion, the conviction that human language is irrelevant and that whatever lies outside human experience has its own idiom, is found in some of the last poems, including "This Region November," a posthumously published poem describing the language of the trees, which "sway, deeply and loudly, in an effort / So much less than feeling, so much less than speech" (*OP*, 140). "Things" speak "on the level of that which is not yet knowledge: A revelation not yet intended." The poem designates the north wind the voice of otherness, a mysterious pre-verbal force that is "like / a critic of God, the world / And human nature" (*OP*, 140). It suggests that reality has a voice that the speaker has never heard. This alien force, which is a sentience, is visible to him by what it displaces but is not understandable. The poem is ominous in tone and defines the circle in such a way as to exclude the poet at the end; his slow progress over a lifetime toward the understanding he so desires leaves him aware of the unintelligibility of the real. The poem asks, Has the poet, in speaking his own speech, missed the words of the real? Are the words of the real audible, and if they can be heard, can they be understood? These questions preoccupied Stevens as he drew toward the end of his creative life.

Perhaps a less ambiguous farewell poem, at least in its tone, is "The River of Rivers in Connecticut," which Stevens placed as the penultimate poem of *The Collected Poems*. The "great river" that is "this side of Stygia" is described as "a gayety, / Flashing and flashing in the sun" (*CP*, 533). The river is an exhilaration, a life source, and it is so powerful that no ferryman can cross it. "He could not bend against its propelling force." This life-river seems to be compared with the death-river Styx, which is not described and is secondary to it. Barbara Fisher notes that in this farewell poem, replete with names important to Stevens's private and public life, it is as though "one has the impression of an entire lifetime 'flashing and flashing in the sun' like pictures going by" (Fisher, 128–55). It is the river that takes over the entire plenum, this river exalted by the title "River of Rivers." If it flows "nowhere," it is because that nowhere is everywhere. It has presence, like the nothing that is there for the Snow Man of *Harmonium* to see.

According to Fisher, " 'River of Rivers' is a culminating work, abundant in spirit, grave and gay and moving as the river it describes. It is Stevens's final great psalm, its music deep and lovely and many-leveled. Indeed, it is the comprehensive genius of this poem to join its opening with the sacred river of Psalm 46, a prototype of sacred rivers: 'There is a river, the streams whereof shall make glad the city of God, the holy place of the most high'" (Fisher, 148–49). She describes the river as encoding divinity for Stevens. "It embodies the phenomenology of a religious form" (152). This poem, then, can be read as a representation of

Stevens's final belief. It is more indirect and less statemental than the fifth section of "The Sail of Ulysses," in which he lays the issue so bare that he was embarrassed for the poem and deleted the lines in later revision. Direct statement was never for Stevens true poetry, at least not in the common language. But the conclusions he presents so directly here are the hidden kernels of other late poems.

> We come
> To knowledge when we come to life.
> Yet always there is another life,
> A life beyond this present knowing,
> A life lighter than this present splendor,
> Brighter, perfected, and distant away,
> Not to be reached but to be known,
> Not an attainment of the will
> But something illogically received,
> A divination, a letting down
> From loftiness, misgivings dazzlingly
> Resolved in dazzling discovery.

This is the Paradiso that remains in the "enclosures of hypotheses" of "Prologues to What Is Possible." It is, finally, what is possible.

> We shall have gone beyond the symbols
> To that which they symbolized, away
> From the rumors of the speech-full domes,
> To the chatter that is the true legend,
> Like glitter ascended into fire. (*OP*,101)

These last poems define Stevens's ultimate contradiction: that one tries without success to achieve genuine knowledge through intense efforts and creating and decreating the world, and yet such knowledge is there, coming of itself to the exhausted thinker. This position is phenomenological, Husserlian, mystical, and congruent with Stevens's decision to take a final leap of faith. In choosing Catholic Christianity as the rock to leap to, he was only adding the contemplated but never-written fourth criterion for his supreme fiction: "It must be human." His interrogation of all structures left him with the intangible unprovable. It would seem that he came to believe literally what he said in a more general sense in "The Noble Rider and the Sound of Words: "Little of what we have believed has been true. Only the prophecies are true" (*NA*, 21).

Chapter Eight

Conclusion: Stevens and Criticism, Stevens and History

Critical assessment of Stevens's position in American literature has been a matter of controversy from the outset, and the essential Stevens remains elusive. The poems and letters offer support for nearly all positions. How is one to approach the work of a poet who asserts clearly in one letter that the "supreme fiction" is poetry, and in another just as clearly that it is not? Only a critic trying to establish Stevens's contradictory nature would trouble to quote both. Stevens was gracious to his critics, often agreeing with them to a point, but saying, "Yes, this: but not entirely this, not only this." It is the same principle as the recurrent "and yet . . ." of his poems. He did not wish to be the inhabitant of others' structures any more than he wished to imprison himself.

Stevens first entered the literary scene during the World War I era, a high point of artistic energy and innovation, carrying with him the baggage of the nineteenth century.[1] After his first works appeared in the experimental journal *Trend* and in the innovative *Poetry* and *Others*, critics initially perceived him as both an experimentalist and an elitist. He and other modernist poets formed a coterie or school (they actually considered calling themselves the postdecadents)[2] on one side affiliated with the Dadaist iconoclasts and on the other with verbal dandyism, "pure" art, and an elitist elegance reminiscent of Oscar Wilde (Schaum, 12). It is this poetry that was first panned or praised by Stevens's contemporaries, even before the appearance of his first book. Pound described Stevens as "a schoolgirl straining for originality,"[3] whereas others found his brand of innovation provocative and exhilarating. Pound was among the few well-known commentators initially to disparage Stevens, and the discrepancy between the views of the two poets remained a constant throughout their lives, an odd circumstance considering how much they shared. But Pound's point remained, although it could be seen as equally true of his own work: the effort to be original was clearly visible.

In *Wallace Stevens and the Critical Schools* (1988), Melita Schaum has traced some of the conflicting appropriations and assessments among

Stevens critics since his work was first publicly discussed in the second decade of the century. Conrad Aiken and Louis Untermeyer argued, in the *New Republic*, issues of Europeanism versus Americanism and ivory-tower poetry versus socially conscious work. Basing his theory on universal standards and distinguishing it from passing social concerns, Aiken advocated "absolute poetry" that "delivers no message, is imbued with no doctrine, a poetry that exists only for the sake of magic,—magic of beauty on the one hand, magic of reality on the other, but both struck at rather through a play of implication than through matter-of-fact statement. This sort of poetry is of course unmoral and unsociological."[4] Aiken championed Stevens as a fine poet by this definition, which stands in contrast to that of Louis Untermeyer, who rejected Stevens as an art-for-art's-sake technician, a sort of Andrea del Sarto of poetry who was capable of "mere verbal legerdemain."[5] Untermeyer sought a sense of social involvement in poetry and believed that art should be "community expression" of a direct nature.

All of the early critics reacted to Stevens's irony and wit. The early modernists praised him, with the exclusion of Pound, who, as suggested by his comment above, seemed to find him prissy and forced. John Gould Fletcher, Llewelyn Powys, Maxwell Bodenheim, and others found pleasure in the ironic ambiguities of Stevens's first work. Those who placed a heavy moral and ethical burden on poetry disliked him, either finding his complexities an annoying withdrawal from the task of communicating or seeing him as a hyper-self-aware Pierrot dancing around a zero center (as Paul Rosenfeld saw him in a review quoted by Schaum):[6] "Hence his ideal self, the cruelly murdered I-the-magnificent, incapable of revealing itself in all its princeliness, gains satisfaction in the shape of revenge. It takes the exaltations of the subject emotional self, and very archly turns them into parody. Of melancholy soliloquy and philosophical dudgeon it makes a silvery music signifying nothing" (quoted by Schaum, 52). Thus, the early critics agreed that irony and ambiguity are central to Stevens's work, but they disagreed about the value of the poetry, depending mostly on whether they thought poetry should be primarily in the service of beauty or of society.

Stevens's early poetry fit the New Critics' approach to poetry perfectly; they sought the qualities of "complexity, inclusivity, and synthesis" (Schaum, 66) in art, the very qualities Stevens seemed most to offer. The New Critics reacted negatively to the Untermeyer school, finding it simplistic, although they too held to an underlying pattern (in some cases, a Christian one) in their analysis of art. I. A. Richards, a critic Stevens read, quoted, and admired and one of the founders of this critical method, claimed that a poem stimulates the reader's sense of harmony by activating opposing impulses through the complex, ambiguous language of the poem. The early New Critics believed Stevens's apparent search for order in chaos was congruent with theirs, and they discussed Stevens frequently in their attempts to define poetry. In turn, he was affected by their theory and their practice; they dominated the critical scene for more than two decades.

In the 1960s and early 1970s, as the New Criticism was losing its power, book-length studies generally focused on a particular image group or thematic center, or on a direction that could be observed through a chronological reading of *The Collected Poems*. Many of the discussions provided close readings interwoven with links between poems, relevant biography, and comments on progression. The best of these books are still the major entrée to Stevens for students and others engaged in preliminary research. A. Walton Litz's *The Introspective Voyager* (1972), Joseph Riddel's *The Clairvoyant Eye* (1965), and Helen Vendler's *On Extended Wings* (1969), among others, are frequently the first stops in investigations of Stevens. These books are influenced by the New Criticism but not limited to the New Critics' methodology, although they do rest on the comfortable assumptions, unquestioned in the 1970s, that literature exists as a separate form from other writings, that there are standards for it (however arguable), and that it is subject to methodical analysis (however much the methods may vary).

Stevens's later work was less favorably received by the same New Critics who had earlier praised it, as they could no longer find the desired sense of closure or reconciliation of opposites in it. Schaum comments, "This confusion about Stevens's poetry echoes the ambivalence of those 'metaphysical' critics seeking reflections of world order, who similarly saw Stevens as either consummate penetrator or hedonistic connoisseur of chaos. . . . All these advocates of wholeness and closure—whether formal, metaphysical, or humanistic—found Stevens's poetry a restless bedfellow with their poetics of inclusivity and completion" (99). It was for the 1980s deconstructionists to embrace him as a true 'connoisseur of chaos,' as their predecessor in decentering verbal activity.

The theory-grounded critics in the late 1970s and 1980s tended to deemphasize *Harmonium* and *Ideas of Order*, focusing instead on the longer poems that had as yet either mostly escaped critical scrutiny or been condemned for their lack of the closure demanded by New Critical principles. In fact, Stevens would come to be perceived as a deconstructionist himself. Of the postmodern approach to Stevens, Schaum notes, "There was a questioning of the nature and function of language beyond traditional formalistic and semantic analyses and toward a concept of the mediate, insufficient, self-undermining nature of language" (100–101). It is easy to see Stevens as expressing such a position in his later work, in which he questions the reliability of language and the ability of static language to represent flexible and discontinuous truth.

Roy Harvey Pearce's first work on Stevens focused on Stevens's notion of decreation as central to his poetry. He saw the poems as an energetic grappling with the dilemma that one cannot know reality uncolored by perception. Language is itself a distortion of reality, and Pearce described Stevens as trying to "abstract language out of existence" (Schaum, 107), thus removing the barrier it places between the perceiver and the perceived. The imagination's triumph places the maker in a godlike role. The deconstructionists gave a much less positive reading to the longer poems. J. Hillis Miller found Stevens to be a poet of the abyss, creating and decreating without closure and without advance. Miller exhibited a poet of existential angst, one who believed that "the evaporation of the gods, leaving a barren man in a barren land, is the basis of all Stevens' poetry" (Schaum, 111). Driven by his sense of the incompatibility between mind and world, this Stevens cyclically denudes and reclothes the real, "the way / A season changes color to no end" (*CP*, 416).

The 1980s saw a number of additional theory-informed perspectives, some of which came from earlier critics who had changed their views with the new developments in criticism. Joseph Riddel, for example, now claimed Stevens for postmodernism; Pearce's views too changed somewhat in this direction. Harold Bloom made Stevens the inheritor and progenitor of the American poetic tradition, following in the traces of Emerson and Whitman. Bloom places Stevens in the grid of his idiosyncratic theory of "poetic crossings," critical personal experiences that are overcome through a rhetorical shifting of gears. Thus, Bloom's 1977 book on Stevens needs to be read in context with his *The Anxiety of Influence* (1973), *A Map of Misreading* (1975), and other critical works.

Critics thought of as mainly theorists are also attracted to Stevens. Paul Bové, whose theory derives in part from Jacques Derrida, found Stevens an agile poet of the void. "The Snow Man," a favorite poem for so many critics, becomes a parable of nihilism rather than of minimalism: "After reduction, the listener 'beholds' more clearly that his

pathetic identification with a seemingly concrete other is a fiction at
the root of which lies 'nothing'" (Schaum, 148–49). The Marxist direction of the criticism of the theorist Frank Lentriccia is more focused on
Stevens's attitudes toward others and things; his glittery, persuasive
book *Ariel and the Police* (1988) traces attitudes toward people and
property in the works of Stevens, Henry James, and Michel Foucault.
His readings of Stevens support his general positions on poetry and
possessions. Other critics wish to use Stevens as a means of defining his
culture. For instance, Robert Emmett Monroe comments, "In some
ways, Stevens seems the most promising major poet of his generation
for a cultural analysis, the most representative poet of his society."[7]

The 1990s Stevens also reflects the critical concerns of the decade.
The interest in a historical Stevens predates the New Historicism, of
course; Glen MacLeod's *Wallace Stevens and Company: The Harmonium
Years* (1985) provides a fine analysis of the relationship between
Stevens and the American art world of the first two decades of the century. (His more recent book, *Wallace Stevens and Modern Art* [1993], fills
in the details of Stevens's relationships with the art movements and
with particular artists and works.) The later books have a different
notion of history and a different goal. James Longenbach and Alan
Filreis look at Stevens's reception of world events and his appropriation
of the national and local into his poetry. Informed by New Historical
critical principles, both these studies give us a Stevens who is very
much a product of and bound to the real world of ordinary life and
common concerns. Other critics examine law and insurance as they
relate to Stevens's poetry. In general, the approach taken by the 1990s
critics may be a corrective to the split between dichotomies that characterized earlier analysis. These critics tend to define a Stevens who is
inseparable from his historical context. The persuasion quotient of
these discussions seems to be based on the agility of the proponent, not
the impregnability of the position.

Not a part of any school of theory or movement in criticism, what
might be called philosophically based studies have appeared in all time
periods. These studies, which provide a Stevens with an ahistorical
dimension, include Hines's 1976 reading of Stevens as a phenomenologist, Richard Bevis's understanding of the poetry as in the tradition of
Eastern mysticism (1988), and Joseph Carroll's tracing of Stevens's
"new romantic" that ends in Catholicism (1987). Also included are
other studies, book-length and otherwise, that follow the traces of particular philosophical interests and readings in Stevens's poetry.

Nietzschean parallels are the focus of B. J. Leggett's *Wallace Stevens: The Nietzschean Intertext* (1992), and Nietzsche looms large also in David Jarraway's *The Metaphysician in the Dark: Wallace Stevens and the Question of Belief* (1993). In keeping with the 1990s blurring of the lines between genres and even between disciplines, Stevens has been appropriated by practitioners in other fields. James Gleick quotes him in his popular book on chaos theory as a foresighted physical theorist: "Stevens's poetry often imparts a vision of tumult in atmosphere and water. It also conveys a faith about the invisible forms that order takes in nature, a belief 'that, in the shadowless atmosphere, / The knowledge of things lay round but unperceived.' When Libchaber and some other experimenters in the 1970s began looking into the motion of fluids, they did so with something approaching this subversive poetic intent. They suspected a connection between motion and universal form" (Gleick, 196). It is unsurprising that literary critics who are dipping into chaos theory and other forms of science to find new paradigms for literary criticism, such as N. Katherine Hayles, should quote the ultimate Connoisseur of Chaos,[8] but his appearance in works on physics itself shows the spread of his influence.

That so many are eager to claim Stevens is an index of his power. That none can do so conclusively demonstrates his uncanny ability to play Houdini in the shackles of critical theory and practice. It is not the case that it merely adds to the weight of any position to annex a giant; the Marxists are not bidding much for Eliot, or the Christians for Pound. Stevens's poems express with his inimitably clear ambiguity the human desire for "what will suffice"; critics and readers listen and find in the intensity of his need a mirror of their own.

William Burney commented in 1968, "Stevens' place is . . . clearly in the tradition of existentialist romanticism. The fertile fact or sensation is primary, everything, including the existence or nonexistence of God, follows from that." He adds that, for Stevens, "the only order worth looking for is the order of chaos itself" (177). That he should have found this order in the Roman Catholic Church is either fundamental or irrelevant, depending on one's perspective. Burney's placement stands, and the flexible yet suggestive category is one that notes both the idealism of Stevens's work (as expressed in the tradition of Emerson, Whitman, and William James) and its intense preoccupation with change and evanescence. Stevens the existential romantic is likely to outlast, or at least to coexist with, all others, although his very idealism is based on the possibility of a true engagement with the actual that would provide a meeting ground for real and ideal. His appeal is his inexhaustibility: each critical reader brings to Stevens his or her own search and finds his or her own process and engagement in the poetry. Stevens's hidden intent seems to include our appropriations of him, as well as his of us, in the strenuous effort toward knowledge.

> We must endure our thoughts all night, until
> The bright obvious stands motionless in cold. (*CP*, 351)

Notes and References

Chapter One

1. See Lucy Beckett's *Wallace Stevens* (London: Cambridge University Press, 1974), hereafter cited in the text; Leonora Woodman's *Stanza My Stone: Wallace Stevens and the Hermetic Tradition* (West Lafayette, Ind.: Purdue University Press, 1983); and Adelaide Kirby Morris's *Wallace Stevens: Imagination and Faith* (Princeton, N.J.: Princeton University Press, 1974).

2. Wallace Stevens, *The Collected Poems of Wallace Stevens* (New York: Alfred A. Knopf, 1955), 524, hereafter cited in the text as *CP*.

3. Joseph Carroll, *Wallace Stevens' Supreme Fiction: A New Romanticism* (Baton Rouge: Louisiana State University Press, 1987); Barbara Fisher, *Wallace Stevens: The Intensest Rendezvous* (Charlottesville: University Press of Virginia, 1990), hereafter cited in the text.

4. Wallace Stevens, *Letters of Wallace Stevens*, ed. Holly Stevens (New York: Alfred A. Knopf, 1957), 378, hereafter cited in the text as *LWS*.

5. See "Presence of an External Master of Knowledge," in Wallace Stevens, *Opus Posthumous*, ed. Milton Bates (New York: Alfred A. Knopf, 1989), 131, hereafter cited in the text as *OP*.

6. Joan Richardson, *Wallace Stevens: The Early Years, 1879–1923* (New York: Beech Tree Books, 1986), plate following p. 192, hereafter cited in the text as Richardson I.

7. René Taupin, *L'Influence du symbolisme français sur la poésie américaine (de 1910 à 1920)* (Geneva: Slatkine Reprints, 1975), 276.

8. MacLeod, Glen, *Wallace Stevens and Company: The "Harmonium" Years, 1913–1923* (Ann Arbor: UMI Research Press, 1985), 22, hereafter cited in the text.

9. Gorham B. Munson, "The Dandyism of Wallace Stevens," *Dial* 79 (1925): 415.

10. A. Walton Litz, *Introspective Voyager: The Poetic Development of Wallace Stevens* (New York: Oxford University Press, 1972), 44, hereafter cited in the text.

11. Joseph Carroll, *Wallace Stevens' Supreme Fiction: A New Romanticism* (Baton Rouge: Louisiana State University Press, 1987), 49, hereafter cited in the text.

12. See "Susannah," in *The New Oxford Annotated Bible with the Apocrypha*, Revised Standard Version, ed. Herbert G. May and Bruce M. Metzger (New York: Oxford University Press, 1977), app. 213 (*Apocrypha* section numbered separately). Probably composed in the second or first century

B.C., the Susannah story is not present in the original Hebrew and Aramaic text but appears in the ancient Greek and Latin versions of the book of Daniel.

13. See Litz's treatment of "Peter Quince at the Clavier" in *Introspective Voyager*, and also Joseph Riddel's in *The Clairvoyant Eye* (Baton Rouge: Louisiana State University Press, 1965), 79–86.

14. B. J. Leggett, *Early Stevens: The Nietzschean Intertext* (Durham, N.C.: Duke University Press, 1992), 64–67, hereafter cited in the text.

15. Ralph Waldo Emerson, "The Transcendentalist," in *The Complete Works of Ralph Waldo Emerson*, 12 vols. (Boston: Houghton Mifflin, 1904), 1:332–33; quoted by Carroll (57).

16. John Jacob Enck, *Wallace Stevens: Images and Judgments* (Carbondale: Southern Illinois University Press, 1964), 85.

17. Frank Kermode, *Wallace Stevens* (New York: Grove Press, 1961), 55.

18. The plays themselves are in *Opus Posthumous*. Some useful commentary about their nature and their relationship to Stevens's other early work is found in the first chapter of William Burney's *Wallace Stevens* (New York: Twayne Publishers, 1968), hereafter cited in the text.

Chapter Two

1. James Longenbach, *Wallace Stevens: The Plain Sense of Things* (New York: Oxford University Press, 1991), 79, hereafter cited in the text.

2. This letter is in the Huntington Library. See also Peter Brazeau, *Parts of a World: Wallace Stevens Remembered: An Oral Biography* (New York: Random House, 1983), xiii, hereafter cited in the text.

3. Joan Richardson, *Wallace Stevens: The Later Years, 1923–1955* (New York: Beech Tree Books, 1988), 80, hereafter cited in the text as Richardson II.

4. See Leggett (1992), as well as David La Guardia's *Advance on Chaos: The Sanctifying Imagination of Wallace Stevens* (Hanover, N.H.: University Press of New England, for Brown University, 1983) and David Jarraway's *Wallace Stevens and the Question of Belief* (Baton Rouge: Louisiana State University Press, 1993).

5. For a discussion of the marital disappointment, see the chapter "The Woman Won, The Woman Lost," in Milton J. Bates, *Wallace Stevens: A Mythology of Self* (Berkeley: University of California Press, 1985), 49–82.

6. Stanley Burnshaw, "Turmoil in the Middle Ground," *New Masses* (1 October 1935): 42, hereafter cited in the text.

7. *American College Dictionary* (New York: Random House, 1962), 1032.

Chapter Three

1. See Brazeau (37, 89), but also elsewhere throughout the section "At the Hartford" (3–93). Stevens allowed only a few chosen initiates a glimpse of his artistic concerns.

2. In addition to James Longenbach (1991), see Alan Filreis, *Wallace Stevens and the Actual World* (Princeton, N.J.: Princeton University Press, 1991).

3. Theodore Roethke, "Wallace Stevens' Ideas of Order," *New Republic* (15 July 1936): 15.

4. See, for instance, Longenbach (1991, 163–73), and the "Stevens and Politics" issue of the *Wallace Stevens Journal* 13, no. 2 (1989).

5. For a good discussion of Stevens and the politics of the 1930s, see chapter 5, "Restatement of Romance" (155–94), in Bates (1985).

6. Frank Lentriccia, *Ariel and the Police: Michel Foucault, William James, and Wallace Stevens* (Madison: University of Wisconsin Press, 1988).

7. For a sense of the importance of the shopping trips to Stevens and an account of the acquisition of the Buddha, see *LWS* (271, 280, 281, 332, 333, 337) and elsewhere. A series of letters that focuses almost exclusively on the proxy shopping is Wallace Stevens's "Letters to Ferdinand Reyer," ed. Holly Stevens, *Hudson Review* 44, no. 3 (Autumn 1991): 381–409.

Chapter Four

1. Mary Katherine Stevens's war letters are in the Stevens Archive in the Huntington Library.

2. Wallace Stevens, *The Necessary Angel: Essays on Reality and the Imagination* (New York: Alfred A. Knopf, 1951), 12, hereafter cited in the text as *NA*.

3. See Woodman (1983) and Morris (1974) for good analyses of Stevens's alchemy.

4. For a persuasive interpretation of "Man on the Dump" that sees the poem as even more Christian in perspective than this study does, see Carroll (1987, 156).

5. James Gleick, *Chaos: Making a New Science* (New York: Viking Penguin, 1987), 196, hereafter cited in the text.

6. Walt Whitman, "Song of Myself," in *Complete Poetry and Selected Prose*, ed James E. Miller, Jr. (Boston: Houghton Mifflin, 1959), 68.

Chapter Five

1. The letter is in the Stevens Archive in the Huntington Library.

2. The letter is in the Stevens Archive in the Huntington Library.

3. See Charles Doyle, *Wallace Stevens: The Cultural Heritage* (London and Boston: Routledge and Kegan, 1985), for the various reviews.

4. The most compelling of the several discussions of Dante and Stevens is Fisher (1990).

5. For a discussion of the mesocosmic figure in literature, see Michael Routh, "The Story of All Things: Faulkner's Yoknapatawpha County Cosmology" (dissertation, University of Wisconsin, 1973), 192–225.

6. Charles Baudelaire, "Au lecteur," in *Les Fleurs du mal* (Paris: Garnier

Frères, 1961), hereafter cited in the text as *Fleurs*. The Baudelaire line reads, "Hypocrite lecteur! Mon semblable, mon frère!"

7.   Christopher Marlowe, *The Tragical History of the Life and Death of Doctor Faustus*, act 5, sc. 2, l. 137.

8.   See Longenbach (1991, 163–73), and also Robert Emmett Monroe's "Figuration and Society in 'Owl's Clover,'" *Wallace Stevens Journal* 13, no. 2 (Fall 1988): 127–49.

9.   Charles Baudelaire, "Curiosités Esthétiques," *Oeuvres Complètes* (Paris: Garnier, 1931), 910–40. For a fine discussion of the Baudelairean elements in Stevens, see Michel Benamou, *Wallace Stevens and the Symbolist Imagination* (Princeton, N.J.: Princeton University Press, 1972), 47–67.

10.   A treatment of specific Baudelairean motifs in the poem is Raymond Poggenburg's "Baudelaire and Stevens: 'L'Esthétique du Mal,'" *South Atlantic Bulletin* 33 (November 1968): 14–18.

11.   For a different perspective on the meaning of the dedication, see Harold Bloom's *Wallace Stevens: The Poems of Our Climate* (Ithaca, N.Y.: Cornell University Press, 1977), 167–218.

12.   Helen Vendler, " 'Notes toward a Supreme Fiction': Allegorical Personae," *Wallace Stevens Journal* 17, no. 2 (Fall 1993): 147–61.

13.   The New Historicism critics, particularly Longenbach, use the last section to read "Notes" as a war poem, but tracing the letters concerning the composition of the poem and its presentation may suggest that the section was an attempt to connect his work with the current situation, that is, to avoid further accusations of escapism.

Chapter Six

1.   See *Secretaries of the Moon: The Letters of Wallace Stevens and José Rodriguez Feo*, ed. Beverly Coyle and Alan Filreis (Durham, N.C.: Duke University Press, 1986).

2.   For the most extensive information about Stevens's conversion, see Sister Bernetta Quinn's essay "Wallace Stevens: 'The Peace of the Last Intelligence,'" in *Renascence* 41 (Summer 1989): 191–210. See also Milton Bates, "Wallace Stevens' Final Yes: A Reply to Sister Bernetta Quinn," in the same issue (205–8).

3.   See the Rev. Cassian Yuhaus's letter to Joseph Schwartz in *Renascence* 41 (Summer 1989): 209–10.

4.   Thomas Hines, *The Later Poetry of Wallace Stevens: Phenomenological Parallels with Husserl and Heidegger* (Lewisburg, Penn.: Bucknell University Press, 1976).

5.   "The nature of god is a circle of which the centre is everywhere and the circumference is nowhere" is a passage of unknown origin, but it is quoted in the thirteenth-century *Le Roman de la Rose*.

Chapter Seven

1.   Compare the endings of Richardson (1988), Carroll (1987), and Longenbach (1991) for an idea of this disparity.

2.   Father Arthur Hanley, St. Bridget's Rectory, Cheshire, Connecticut, letter to Janet McCann, 24 July 1977.

3.   Janet McCann and others were told by a spokesperson at St. Bridget's that Father Hanley was overburdened by researchers.

4.   *Wallace Stevens Reads His Poetry*, Caedmon recording, TC 1086, 1954.

5.   C. G. Jung, *The Archetypes and the Collective Unconscious*, tr. R. F. C. Hull (Princeton, N.J.: Princeton University Press, 1959), 157.

6.   Edmund Wilson, "Santayana at the Convent of the Blue Nuns," *New Yorker* (6 April 1946): 59–67.

Chapter Eight

1.   For a full discussion of Stevens's early artistic influences, see the first two chapters of MacLeod (1985).

2.   Melita Schaum, *Wallace Stevens and the Critical Schools* (Tuscaloosa: University of Alabama Press, 1988), 1–3, hereafter cited in the text.

3.   Quoted in Ellen Williams, *Harriet Monroe and the Poetry Renaissance* (Urbana: University of Illinois Press, 1977), 222; originally published in *Little Review* (June 1918): 17.

4.   Conrad Aiken, "The Ivory Tower—I," *New Republic* (10 May 1919): 60.

5.   Louis Untermeyer, "The Ivory Tower—II," *New Republic* (10 May 1919): 61.

6.   Paul Rosenfeld, *Men Seen: Twenty-Four Modern Authors* (New York: Dial Press, 1925), 156–57.

7.   Robert Emmett Monroe, "Figuration and Society in 'Owl's Clover,'" *Wallace Stevens Journal* 31, no. 2 (Fall 1989): 127.

8.   Kathleen N. Hayles, *Chaos and Order: Complex Dynamics in Literature and Science* (Chicago: University of Chicago Press, 1991), i.

Bibliography

Primary Sources

Poems and Plays

Harmonium. New York: Alfred A. Knopf, 1923.
Ideas of Order. New York: Alcestis Press, 1935.
Ideas of Order. New York: Alfred A. Knopf, 1936.
Owl's Clover. New York: Alcestis Press, 1936.
The Man with the Blue Guitar and Other Poems. New York: Alfred A. Knopf, 1937.
Parts of a World. New York: Alfred A. Knopf, 1942.
Notes toward a Supreme Fiction. Cummington, Mass.: Cummington Press, 1942.
Description without Place. Sewanee, Tenn.: University Press, 1945.
Transport to Summer. New York: Alfred A. Knopf, 1947.
A Primitive Like an Orb. New York: Gotham Book Mart, 1948.
The Auroras of Autumn. New York: Alfred A. Knopf, 1950.
The Collected Poems of Wallace Stevens. New York: Alfred A. Knopf, 1954.
Opus Posthumous. New York: Alfred A. Knopf, 1957.
The Palm at the End of the Mind: Selected Poems and a Play. Edited by Holly Stevens. New York: Alfred A. Knopf, 1971.

Prose

Three Academic Pieces. Cummington, Mass: Cummington Press, 1947.
Two or Three Ideas. Hartford, Conn.: College English Association, 1951.
The Necessary Angel. New York: Alfred A. Knopf, 1951.
Opus Posthumous. New York: Alfred A. Knopf, 1957.
Letters of Wallace Stevens. Selected and edited by Holly Stevens. New York: Alfred A. Knopf, 1967.
Secretaries of the Moon: The Letters of Wallace Stevens and José Rodriguez Feo. Edited by Beverly Coyle and Alan Filreis. Durham, N.C.: Duke University Press, 1986.
Sur Plusieurs Beaux Sujects: Wallace Stevens's Commonplace Book: A Facsimile and Transcription. Edited by Milton J. Bates. Stanford, Calif.: Stanford University Press, 1989.

Secondary Sources

Journal

Wallace Stevens Journal. Edited by John Serio. 1977– .

Bibliographies and Concordance

Edelstein, J. M. *Wallace Stevens: A Descriptive Bibliography*. Pittsburgh:
    University of Pittsburgh Press, 1973.
Morse, Samuel French, Jackson R. Bryer, and Joseph N. Riddel. *Wallace Stevens
    Checklist and Bibliography of Stevens Criticism*. Denver: Alan Swallow, 1963.
Serio, John. *Wallace Stevens: An Annotated Secondary Bibliography*. Pittsburgh:
    University of Pittsburgh Press, 1994.
Walsh, Thomas F. *Concordance to the Poetry of Wallace Stevens*. University Park:
    Pennsylvania State University Press, 1963.

Essay Collections

Axelrod, Steven Gould, and Helen Deese, eds. *Critical Essays on Wallace Stevens*.
    Boston: G. K. Hall, 1988.
Blessington, Francis C., and Guy Rotalla, eds. *Essays on Modern Poetry in Honor of
    Samuel French Morse*. Boston: Northeastern University Press, 1983.
Borroff, Marie, ed. *Wallace Stevens: A Collection of Critical Essays*. Englewood
    Cliffs, N.J.: Prentice-Hall, 1963.
Doggett, Frank, and Robert Buttel, eds. *Wallace Stevens: A Celebration*.
    Princeton, N.J.: Princeton University Press, 1980.
Doyle, Charles, ed. *Wallace Stevens: The Critical Heritage*. London: Routledge and
    Kegan Paul, 1985.
Ehrenpreis, Irvin, ed. *Wallace Stevens: A Critical Anthology*. Middlesex, Eng.:
    Penguin, 1972.
Gelpi, Albert, ed. *Wallace Stevens: The Poetics of Modernism*. Cambridge, Eng.:
    Cambridge University Press, 1985.
Leggett, B. J., and John Serio, eds. *Teaching Wallace Stevens: Practical Essays*.
    Knoxville: University of Tennessee Press, 1994.
Pearce, Roy Harvey, and J. Hillis Miller, eds. *The Act of the Mind*. Baltimore:
    Johns Hopkins University Press, 1965.
Schaum, Melita, ed. *Wallace Stevens and the Feminine*. Tuscaloosa: University of
    Alabama Press, 1993.

Books

Baird, James. *The Dome and the Rock: Structure in the Poetry of Wallace Stevens*.
    Baltimore: Johns Hopkins University Press, 1968. Traces the develop-
    ment of Stevens's major concerns—centering on the motifs of dome and
    rock—throughout his work. Still valuable and often cited.

Bates, Milton J. *Wallace Stevens: A Mythology of Self*. Berkeley: University of California Press, 1985. "How one poet transcended biography by transforming it into fables of identity." Excellent use of biographical materials.

Beckett, Lucy. *Wallace Stevens*. London: Cambridge University Press, 1974. Sound basic study.

Benamou, Michael. *Wallace Stevens and the Symbolist Imagination*. Princeton, N.J.: Princeton University Press, 1972. Startlingly insightful early study of the echoes of Baudelaire, Mallarmé, et al. in Stevens's work.

Berger, Charles. *Forms of Farewell: The Late Poetry of Wallace Stevens*. Madison: University of Wisconsin Press, 1985. Considers Stevens's last decade as a poet, with emphasis on his war poems and poems about the approach of death.

Bevis, William W. *Mind of Winter: Wallace Stevens, Meditation, and Literature*. Pittsburgh: University of Pittsburgh Press, 1988. Examines Stevens's poetic as it corresponds with the history of Eastern meditative practice.

Blessing, Richard. *Wallace Stevens's 'Whole Harmonium.'* Syracuse, N.Y.: Syracuse University Press, 1970. Basic study.

Bloom, Harold. *Wallace Stevens: The Poems of Our Climate*. Ithaca, N.Y.: Cornell University Press, 1977. Interprets Stevens in the light of Bloom's theory of literature; Aristotelian slant.

Brazeau, Peter. *Parts of a World: Wallace Stevens Remembered: An Oral Biography*. New York: Random House, 1983. Contains texts of recordings with those who knew Stevens. Divided into sections on Stevens as insurance lawyer, family man, and poet. Indispensable.

Brogan, Jacqueline Vaught. *Stevens and Simile: A Theory of Language*. Princeton, N.J.: Princeton University Press, 1986. Examines Stevens's poetic language with reference to Derrida, Frye, Aquinas, and others.

Bové, Paul. *Destructive Poetics: Heidegger and Modern American Poetry*. New York: Columbia University Press, 1980. Deconstructionist criticism that radically reinterprets Stevens.

Burney, William A. *Wallace Stevens*. New York: Twayne, 1968. Useful close readings and general thematic analysis.

Buttel, Robert. *Wallace Stevens: The Making of "Harmonium."* Princeton, N.J.: Princeton University Press, 1967. Solid early study of *Harmonium*.

Byers, Thomas B. *What I Cannot Say: Self, Word, and World in Whitman, Stevens, and Merwin*. Urbana: University of Illinois Press, 1989. Epistemological study of the three poets.

Carroll, Joseph. *Wallace Stevens's Supreme Fiction: A New Romanticism*. Baton Rouge: Louisiana State University Press, 1987. Thorough, sound study that focuses on the metaphysical strain in Stevens.

Cook, Eleanor. *Poetry, Word-Play, and Word-War in Wallace Stevens*. Princeton, N.J.: Princeton University Press, 1987. Traces Stevens's riddles, puns, and grammatical word games through close readings and intertextual analysis.

Coyle, Beverly. *A Thought to Be Rehearsed: Aphorism in the Poetry of Wallace Stevens*. Ann Arbor: UMI Research Press, 1983. Useful and original analysis of the use of aphorisms during the phases of Stevens's career.

Dickie, Margaret. *Lyric Contingencies: Emily Dickinson and Wallace Stevens.* Philadelphia: University of Pennsylvania Press, 1991. Theory-based study of Stevens and Dickinson as lyricists.

Doggett, Frank. *Wallace Stevens's Poetry of Thought.* Baltimore: Johns Hopkins University Press, 1966. This still useful, frequently cited basic guide to Stevens analyzes theme and image.

———. *Wallace Stevens: The Making of the Poem.* Baltimore: Johns Hopkins University Press, 1980. Examination of Stevens's method.

Enck, John Jacob. *Wallace Stevens: Images and Judgments.* Carbondale: Southern Illinois University Press, 1964. Classic study of imagery.

Filreis, Alan. *Wallace Stevens and the Actual World.* Princeton, N.J.: Princeton University Press, 1991. Places Stevens in cultural history.

———. *Modernism from Right to Left: Wallace Stevens, the Thirties, and Literary Radicalism.* Cambridge, Eng.: Cambridge University Press, 1994. A historicist approach to Stevens and politics.

Fisher, Barbara M. *Wallace Stevens: The Intensest Rendezvous.* Charlottesville: University Press of Virginia, 1990. Original and persuasive readings showing Dantean parallels.

Fuchs, Daniel. *The Comic Spirit of Wallace Stevens.* Durham, N.C.: Duke University Press, 1963. On Stevens's humor and wit.

Grey, Thomas C. *The Wallace Stevens Case: Law and the Practice of Poetry.* Cambridge, Mass.: Harvard University Press, 1991. Reunites Stevens's two careers.

Halliday, Mark. *Stevens and the Interpersonal.* Princeton, N.J.: Princeton University Press, 1991. On the importance of personal relationships in Stevens's poems.

Hertz, David Michael. *Angels of Reality: Emerson Unfoldings in Wright, Stevens, and Ives.* Carbondale: Southern Illinois University Press, 1993. Emerson's concepts of nature and organicism and a theory of interartistic influence. Unusual.

Hines, Thomas J. *The Later Poetry of Wallace Stevens: Phenomenological Parallels with Husserl and Heidegger.* Lewisburg, Penn.: Bucknell University Press, 1976. Convincing treatment of Stevens as phenomenologist.

Holmes, Barbara. *The Decomposer's Art: Ideas of Music in the Poetry of Wallace Stevens.* New York: Peter Lang, 1990. Influence of musical terms and composers on Stevens's work.

Jarraway, David. *The Metaphysician in the Dark: Wallace Stevens and the Question of Belief.* Baton Rouge: Louisiana State University Press, 1993. Theory-based study of Stevens's various definitions of belief throughout the poems, and their sources.

Kermode, Frank. *Wallace Stevens.* New York: Grove Press, 1961. Brief, still useful classic study.

Kessler, Edward. *Images of Wallace Stevens*. New Brunswick, N.J.: Rutgers University Press, 1971. Covers the major themes and images.

La Guardia, David. *Advance on Chaos: The Sanctifying Imagination of Wallace Stevens*. Hanover, N.H.: University Press of New England for Brown University, 1983. The influence of Emerson, William James, and others on Stevens's thought.

Leggett, B. J. *Wallace Stevens and Poetic Theory: Conceiving the Supreme Fiction*. Chapel Hill: University of North Carolina Press, 1987. Demonstrates Stevens's application of the work of Mauron, Adams, Focillon, and other theorists to his own poetic.

———. *Wallace Stevens: The Nietzschean Intertext*. Durham, N.C.: Duke University Press, 1992. Clear and innovative discussion of intertextuality and analysis of Nietzschean intertexts.

Lensing, George. *Wallace Stevens: A Poet's Growth*. Baton Rouge: Louisiana State University Press, 1986. Insightful discussion of Stevens's development; also contains useful primary materials from Stevens's notebooks.

Lentriccia, Frank. *The Gaiety of Language: An Essay on the Radical Poetics of William Butler Yeats and Wallace Stevens*. Berkeley: University of California Press, 1968. Theory-based study.

———. *Ariel and the Police: Michel Foucault, William James, and Wallace Stevens*. Madison: University of Wisconsin Press, 1988. An exciting political-historicist reading that places Stevens in "nonpoetic" history as it shows the limitation of current critical methodology.

———. *A Modernist Quartet*. Cambridge, Eng.: Cambridge University Press, 1994. A largely historicist approach to Stevens, Frost, Pound, and Eliot.

Litz, A. Walton. *Introspective Voyager: The Poetic Development of Wallace Stevens*. New York: Oxford University Press, 1972. One of the clearest and most enjoyable general studies.

———. *Wallace Stevens: The Poetry of Earth*. Washington, D.C.: Library of Congress, 1981. Useful essay.

Longenbach, James. *Wallace Stevens: The Plain Sense of Things*. New York: Oxford University Press, 1991. This historical approach analyzes Stevens's poetry as a response to political events, especially wars.

MacLeod, Glen G. *Wallace Stevens and Company: The "Harmonium" Years, 1913–1923*. Ann Arbor: UMI Research Press, 1985. Traces Stevens's crucial involvement with major art and literary movements in the years up to *Harmonium*.

———. *Wallace Stevens and Modern Art: From the Armory Show to Abstract Expressionism*. New Haven, Conn.: Yale University Press, 1993. Intriguing, profusely illustrated discussion of the relationships between Stevens's work and the various art movements and specific artists that interested him.

McMahon, William E. *The Higher Humanism of Wallace Stevens*. Lewiston, N.Y.: Mellen Press, 1991. On Stevens's humanistic philosophy.

Martin, Ronald E. *American Literature and the Destruction of Knowledge: Innovative Writing in the Age of Epistemology*. Durham, N.C.: Duke University Press, 1991. Stevens and several others as experimentalists.

Morse, Samuel French. *Wallace Stevens: Poetry as Life*. New York: Pegasus, 1970. Early study by Stevens's longtime friend, with a biographical emphasis.

Nassar, Eugene. *Wallace Stevens: An Anatomy of Figuration*. Philadelphia: University of Pennsylvania Press, 1965. Study of themes and images.

Morris, Adelaide Kirby. *Wallace Stevens: Imagination and Faith*. Princeton, N.J.: Princeton University Press, 1974. Stevens's use of religious imagery to create a substitute for religion.

Newcomb, John Timberman. *Wallace Stevens and Literary Canons*. Jackson: University Press of Mississippi, 1992. Shows Stevens's reception throughout the changing literary values of the twentieth century.

O'Connor, William Van. *The Shaping Spirit: A Study of Wallace Stevens*. New York: Russell and Russell, 1964. Still useful general study.

Pack, Robert. *Wallace Stevens: An Approach to His Poetry and Thought*. New Brunswick, N.J.: Rutgers University Press, 1958. One of the first general studies, with input from Stevens.

Patke, Rajeev S. *The Long Poems of Wallace Stevens*. New York: Cambridge University Press, 1985. Readings of seven long poems.

Penso, Kia. *Wallace Stevens, "Harmonium," and the Whole of Harmonium*. New York: Archon Books, 1991. Brief and introductory.

Peterson, Margaret. *Wallace Stevens and the Idealist Tradition*. Ann Arbor: UMI Research Press, 1983. Relates Stevens's theory of the imagination to idealist philosophy.

Quinn, Sister Bernetta, O.S.F. *The Metamorphic Tradition in Modern Poetry*. New Brunswick, N.J.: Rutgers University Press, 1955. Provocative essays on Christian elements in Stevens and others.

Quirk, Tom. *Bergson and American Culture: The Worlds of Willa Cather and Wallace Stevens*. Chapel Hill: University of North Carolina Press, 1990. A study in literary history showing the influence of Bergsonian vitalism on Cather and Stevens.

Rehder, Robert. *The Poetry of Wallace Stevens*. New York: St. Martin's Press, 1988. Biographical criticism; a good introductory study.

Richardson, Joan. *Wallace Stevens*, vol. 1, *The Early Years, 1879–1923*; vol. 2, *The Later Years, 1923–1955*. New York: Beech Tree Books, 1986–88. Detailed biography.

Rieke, Alison. *The Senses of Nonsense*. Iowa City: University of Iowa Press, 1992. Stevens considered with Zukovsky, Stein, and James as an experimentalist who uses "nonsense" purposefully.

Riddel, Joseph N. *The Clairvoyant Eye: The Poetry and Poetics of Wallace Stevens.* Baton Rouge: Louisiana State University Press, 1965. Solid, insightful close readings. Old but still useful.

Rotella, Guy. *Reading and Writing Nature: The Poetry of Robert Frost, Wallace Stevens, Marianne Moore, and Elizabeth Bishop.* Boston: Northeastern University Press, 1991. The American ambivalence toward nature as experienced by these writers.

Sawaya, Richard N. *The Skepticism and Animal Faith of Wallace Stevens.* New York: Garland, 1987. On Wallace Stevens and George Santayana.

Schaum, Melita. *Wallace Stevens and the Critical Schools.* Tuscaloosa: University of Alabama Press, 1988. Traces perspectives on Stevens from the 1920s until the late 1980s. Excellent.

Schwartz, Daniel. *Narrative and Representation in the Poetry of Wallace Stevens: 'A Tune Beyond Us, Yet Ourselves.'* New York: St. Martin's Press, 1993. Mimesis in Stevens; clear and direct.

Stevens, Holly. *Souvenirs and Prophecies: The Young Wallace Stevens.* New York: Alfred A. Knopf, 1977. Precise, insightful memoir, with portions of Stevens's early writings.

Sukenick, Ronald. *Wallace Stevens: Musing the Obscure.* New York: New York University Press, 1966. Analysis of major themes and close readings. Still good.

Vendler, Helen. *On Extended Wings: Wallace Stevens's Longer Poems.* Cambridge, Mass.: Harvard University Press, 1969. Classic study of Stevens's long poems.

———. *Words Chosen out of Desire.* Knoxville: University of Tennessee Press, 1984. Examines Stevens's development as a poet with reference to his marriage and expectations of love.

Walker, David. *The Transparent Lyric: Reading and Meaning in the Poetry of Stevens and Williams.* Princeton, N.J.: Princeton University Press, 1984. Shows thematic and formal similarities between the two poets as they require reader participation.

Woodman, Leonora. *Stanza My Stone: Wallace Stevens and the Hermetic Tradition.* West Lafayette, Ind.: Purdue University Press, 1983. Places Stevens within the hermetic tradition but defines him as a monist rather than a dualist.

Index

The Author

Janet McCann has been teaching at Texas A&M University since 1969. She received her Ph.D. from the University of Pittsburgh in 1974. A poet who has published widely in literary and popular magazines, she received a National Endowment for the Arts Creative Writing Fellowship Grant in 1989. She has written articles on Wallace Stevens and on pedagogy, and is also coauthor of the textbook *Creative and Critical Thinking* (1985) and coeditor of the poetry anthology *Odd Angles of Heaven* (1994).

The Editor

Joseph M. Flora earned his B.A. (1956), M.A. (1957), and Ph.D. (1962) in English at the University of Michigan. In 1962 he joined the faculty of the University of North Carolina, where he is now professor of English. His study *Hemingway's Nick Adams* (1984) won the Mayflower Award. He is also author of *Vardis Fisher* (1962), *William Ernest Henley* (1970), *Frederick Manfred* (1974), and *Ernest Hemingway: A Study of the Short Fiction* (1989). He is editor of *The English Short Story* (1985) and coeditor of *Southern Writers: A Biographical Dictionary* (1970), *Fifty Southern Writers before 1900* (1987), *Fifty Southern Writers after 1900* (1987), *Contemporary Fiction Writers of the South* (1993), and *Contemporary Poets, Dramatists, Essayists, and Novelists of the South* (1994).